New Art of Writing

The National Association of Writers' Groups

Compiled by Jayne Osborn

First Published in Great Britain in 2002 by
Barny Books

© National Association of Writers' Groups
All rights reserved

No part of this publication may be reproduced or transmitted in any way or by any means, including electronic storage and retrieval, without prior permission of the publisher.

Published by Barny Books, Hough on the Hill, Grantham, Lincolnshire
Tel: 01400 250246 & Fax: 01400 251737
Produced by: TUCANN*design&print*, 19 High Street, Heighington Lincoln LN4 1RG
Tel & Fax: 01522 790009 - www.tucann.co.uk

Of all the arts in which the wise excel, Nature's chief masterpiece is writing well.
John Sheffield, Duke of Buckingham and Normanby 1648-1721

Contents

Category 1: Free Verse Poem
Harry's Spirit Level - Penelope Alexander .... Page 7

Category 2: Sonnet, Villanelle or Pantoum
A 'Dear John' Villanelle - Jane Lawson .... Page 8

Category 3: Poem for Children
School - John Statham .... Page 9

Category 4: Love Poem
a. The Flirt - Lesley James .... Page 12
b. Obsession - Mary Smythe .... Page 13

Category 5: Poem which can be sung to a well-known tune
Magnificat - Bill Thomas .... Page 14

Category 6: Monologue
Talking Goldfish Head - Alan Murton .... Page 15

Category 7: Open Short Story
The Hat - Gael Shannon .... Page 19

Category 8: Short Story featuring 'Diamonds'
Hidden Depths - Eve Gray .... Page 24

Category 9: Short Story for Children
The Calling - Beth Daniels .... Page 30

Category 10: Non-Fictional Article
Big Night at the Bridgewater - Joyce Neal .... Page 33

Category 11: New 'Sitcom' or 'Soap' for TV
Whoppers - Leona J Bryson .... Page 36

Category 12: Mini Tale
Stuart Randall .... Page 44

Category 13: Novel
Watcher in the Shadows - Judith Cranswick .... Page 45

Category 14:The Denise Robertson Silver Trophy for the Best Group Anthology
ROOM 14 AT 8 O'CLOCK
Richmond Writers Circle .... Page 58

Judges' Comments .... Page 83

Results .... Page 87

Introduction

Welcome to this New Anthology of Writing Gems, which indeed it is.

By the time you are reading this the winners and runners-up from each Competition category will have been presented with their certificates during the Awards Ceremony at our Annual Festival of Writing in Durham. This is the highlight of the year for the National Association of Writers' Groups! We are proud to reproduce the work of each winner here, for your enjoyment.

I would also like to welcome all our new members - Associates and Writers' Groups. The NAWG Competition gives tremendous encouragement to writers to strive for an award, and it is thrilling that some of this year's finalists are among those who only recently joined our ranks.

NAWG continues to go from strength to strength. We have a hardworking Committee who make this happen, a dedicated team of volunteers to whom I say a big 'Thank you' once more.

Happy writing to you all!

Judith Thwaite
NAWG Chairman

From the Competition Administrator

This year saw the introduction of several exciting new categories, which proved to be very popular. Where in the world can you enter fourteen pieces of work in one prestigious competition? - and at no charge!

Needless to say, many new groups and individuals joined the ranks of NAWG this year specifically to take advantage of this marvellous opportunity for writers of all genres. The number of entries, therefore, was high, so the finalists and all those whose work was highly commended can indeed be proud of their achievements.
I'm sure you will enjoy the 'gems' in this anthology. If your name doesn't appear in it, do please try again next year!

Jayne Osborn

Winning entry for category 1
Free Verse Poem
(Judged by Katrina Porteous)

> *A complete poem is one where an emotion has found its thought and the thought has found the words…*
> Robert Frost, American Poet 1874-1963

Harry's Spirit Level

Above the green-eyed bubble
hovers his hardened hand,
taking judgement, whether this wall's straight, or no.
If it lies crooked, he'll not rest till late.
The flower-bed will be made again
And all the bricks unfastened
and relaid, until he knows for sure
they'll each stand firm till kingdom come.

Now held in my hand,
the brass-bound bubble gleams.
Marking the level, warning of crooked ways,
or sloped off edges where no eye can see.
I kept it safe through every move we made.
I take it with me in my mind's pathways.
I need your spirit lined up with me here,
levelling with me where it's good to go.

By Penelope Alexander
(Wellingborough Writers)

Winning entry for category 2
Sonnet, Villanelle or Pantoum
(Judged by Alison Chisholm)

> *For ryhme the rudder is of verses,*
> *With which like ships they steer their courses.*
> Samuel Butler, English Poet 1612-80

A 'Dear John' Villanelle

So much has happened; now it has to end.
I can't go on like this, being controlled.
I know it's something you won't comprehend.

It's best to tell the truth. I can't pretend
our marriage will survive until we're old.
So much has happened; now it has to end.

Things have occurred which I did not intend:
The passion's gone, my feelings have grown cold.
I know it's something you won't comprehend.

You've forced your will on me for years. I tend
to acquiesce and do what I am told.
So much has happened! Now it has to end

because I've met someone, at first a friend,
but now much more. For once I'm feeling bold -
I know it's something you won't comprehend.

The rift between us, far too big to mend,
means that I can escape - I've been paroled!
So much has happened now. It has to end,
I know. - It's something you won't comprehend.

By Jane Lawson (Associate Member)

Winning entry for category 3
Poem For Children
(Judged by Mavis Carter)

Some rhyme a neebor's name to lash;
Some rhyme (vain thought!) for needfu' cash;
Some rhyme to court the countra clash,
An' raise a din;
For me, an aim I never fash;
I rhyme for fun.
Robert Burns, Scottish Poet 1759-96

School

Hello, here's my school, it's a great place to be -
but why should my teacher be frowning at me?

Here is my classroom and there's where I sit,
where Miss says I chatter and fidget a bit.
But that's life and my school is a great place to be,
so why should my teacher be frowning at me?

Just look at my book - I've worked so hard today,
I've not had a moment to gossip and play -
I've been studying hard in my class where I sit,
though Miss says I fidget and chatter a bit.
But that's life and my school is a great place to be,
so why should my teacher be frowning at me?

These are the sums rumour says I got wrong,
which is hard to believe after slaving so long -
just look at my book - I've worked so hard today,
I've not had a moment to gossip and play -

I've been studying hard in my class where I sit,
    though Miss says I fidget and chatter a bit.
But that's life and my school is a great place to be,
    so why should my teacher be frowning at me?

There's the class hamster, escaped once again,
    but it wasn't my fault if they'd let me explain,
for he jumped off my shoulder when scared by the bell,
    being nervous of noise as they know very well.
And these are the sums rumour says I got wrong,
    which is hard to believe after slaving so long -
just look at my book - I've worked so hard today,
    I've not had a moment to gossip and play -
I've been studying hard in my class where I sit,
    though Miss says I fidget and chatter a bit.
But that's life and my school is a great place to be,
    so why should my teacher be frowning at me?

Oh dear - that's the paint teacher saw on Kate's head,
    and I'm rather upset at the things that they said,
for it wasn't on purpose, Wain joggled my arm,
    and when did green spots do a girl any harm?
And oh, the class hamster escaped once again,
    but it wasn't my fault if they'd let me explain,
for he jumped off my shoulder when scared by the bell,
    being nervous of noise as they know very well.
And these are the sums rumour says I got wrong,
    which is hard to believe after slaving so long -
just look at my book - I've worked so hard today,
    I've not had a moment to gossip and play -
I've been studying hard in my class where I sit,
    though Miss says I fidget and chatter a bit.
But that's life and my school is a great place to be,
    so why should my teacher be frowning at me?

But look at the time - that's another day done -
don't the hours gallop by when you're having such fun.
So don't forget all that paint teacher saw on Kate's head,
though I'm rather upset at the things that they said,
for it wasn't on purpose, Wain joggled my arm,
and when did green spots do a girl any harm?
And oh, the class hamster escaped once again,
but it wasn't my fault if they'd let me explain,
for he jumped off my shoulder when scared by the bell,
being nervous of noise as they know very well.
And these are the sums rumour says I got wrong,
which is hard to believe after slaving so long -
just look at my book - I've worked so hard today,
I've not had a moment to gossip and play -
I've been studying hard in my class where I sit,
though Miss says I wriggled and chattered a bit,
but it's been a good day and now home for my tea -
so it's goodbye to my teacher who's smiling at me.

By John Statham (Alsager Writers' Circle)

Joint Winning entries for category 4
Love Poem
(Judged by Dave Etchell)

> *Love (if such a thing there be)*
> *Is all despair, or ecstasy.*
> *Poetry's the feverish fit,*
> *The o'erflowing of unbounded wit.*
> Anne Finch, Lady Winchilsea, English Poet 1661-1720

The Flirt

'Love you' you mouthed and I, almost a stranger,
Laughed, I wasn't yet committed to perdition,
Felt myself immune and saw no danger,
Love was a younger woman's sore condition.

A flirt I thought, a pleasant, practised flirt.
Banter was tossed between us like a ball
Caught just this side of words that lead to hurt,
We were playing with a bomb that meant to fall,

For sometimes in your eyes was honesty
And I'd almost reach a hand to touch your face.
Irresolute, I clutched fidelity
And spared myself adultery's disgrace,

I could not be a whore, a cheat, a liar,
Yet in my dreams I walk to you - through fire.

By Lesley James (Inn Scribers)

Obsession

The broken promise of Spring
is very human,
Daffodils toss in an unkind wind.

When you are promised the world
you have to accept
mist and malevolence,
cold that bites, the barren margins
and a hopeless dawn
along with the sunlit landscape.

You offer me the world:
you offer me your life.
Included in the package
sulk, storm, torpidity
and the heat
of a hundred volcanoes.

I will take the world
and roll it around my life;
take my life and roll it with yours
snowballing the past,
cut grass and moonlight, music
and all those fingerprints.

The irises you gave as a peace offering
shrivel into fists, a bunch
of defensive knuckles.

I will collect the broken promises
in a matchbox until
they spill
over and require a packing case.
I will nail down the lid
and label it 'Pandora - not to be opened!'

by Mary Smythe
(Lewes U3A Writing Workshop)

Winning entry for category 5
Poem which can be sung to a well-known tune
(Judged by John Chambers)

 And this song is considered a perfect gem...
CS Calverley, English writer 1831-84

Magnificat
to the tune of 'The Ash Grove'

1. My soul sings in witness
to God's supreme greatness:
my spirit is glad in my Saviour and Lord,
whose love is so fervent
to this lowly servant
that all generations will call me adored.
For God in his glory
has done great things for me:
his name is kept holy, yet shout it abroad!
To all those who fear him
and turn to revere him
his love and compassion are endlessly poured.

2. God's arm acts in splendour,
his people's defender:
the proud and conceited have scattered and fled.
He throws from the palace
oppression and malice
and lifts up the lowly to glory instead.
All those who had plenty
are turned away empty:
the hungry are welcomed and filled with good bread.
The God of our nation
has brought his salvation
to Abraham's children just as it was said.

By Bill Thomas (Keele Writers' Group)

Winner of category 6
Monologue

Writing, when properly managed (as you can be sure I think mine is), is but a different name for conversation.
Laurence Sterne, English novelist 1713-68

Talking Goldfish Head

"M N O Goldfish!" "O S A R! C D B D Is."
How'd you like to be the subject of a weak racist joke? That's the trouble - nobody ever asks goldfish anything. They might gurgle a bit when they throw another fistful of ants' eggs into the bowl.

Don't they know about my pedigree? It beats an Arab stallion or a Cruft's winner any day. I go back to the Golden Fish of the great Chinese dynasties when we were farmed for the delight of the Sungs, Mings and the Tangs.

I've only been here a few months but what they have done to me shouldn't have happened to a dog let alone to a member of the fish royal family. I didn't mind at first when Darren – that's the little boy who claims that I'm his – got his father to rescue me from that awful fairground. My earliest memories are of being scooped up every morning from a big tin bath with dozens of other goldfish (not all with my superior breeding you understand) and packaged up in clear plastic bags to be hung like some unspeakable criminal from the garish fascia of the shooting gallery.

The noise was awful. I could have tolerated the crack of the air guns with their twisted foresights as countless men tried to impress their girlfriends, wives, children or each other with their marksmanship but that bloody crazy ride next door - it was enough to make a saint swear. The siren shrieked out louder and louder as the machine speeded up but even that didn't drown the screaming of the daft teenagers who'd paid to be thrown from pillar to post. More than one spewed up his cod and chips at the back of our stall. It got more hectic as the pubs shut and I was in greater danger of being hit by a drunk than being won by a clean living parent.

I shudder when I think of those days. We were all shameless as we hung from cup-hooks screwed into the flaking woodwork, swinging there behaving like whores in a French brothel, opening and closing our mouths, teasing, flashing our eyes and swinging our tails. I blush crimson when I realise what a tart I must have seemed.

Still that's all in the past. Darren's Dad hit a lucky streak and he carried me home, clutching my plastic bag tightly in the back of the car; at one time I thought I was going to run short of air but got there safely. It's not a palace but comfortable enough, three beds two receptions and part central heating. My dirty fairground water and I went into a half round plastic bowl balanced on a green plinth on the dining room sideboard. I ask you - plastic - Moi!

I'd hardly time to catch my breath when up swam this lower-class biddy sniffing round me and gurgling with disgust when she found I was female and better bred. We have a goldfish way of recognising breeding but it's too complicated for you to understand.

It turned out that she'd been there a few months and that Darren's older brother, Dean, had won her throwing ping-pong balls at a school fête. I was impressed for a minute until I discovered that ping-pong is a silly game played with bats, not an ancient Oriental gambling game. I was less impressed when I found out that bats are instruments for striking a ball, not nocturnal creatures, that a fête is a posh fun fair and that the jam-jars were from Tesco's.

Eventually I pieced her story together. The boys had squabbled about having only one goldfish, that's why I had been targeted to join Mai Wong in the bowl - it was big enough for two, though we'd both have preferred male company. Dean, imaginative young lad, had called her "Goldie." I prayed long and hard "Please don't let Darren call me "Fishy." Prayers answered, I was called Isis. You might well ask why! Seems that his father is an Oxford man and wanted to redress the balance - seems Dean had named Mai after some second team boat crew or other.

I'm on my own now. Mai went to her ancestors, such as they

might be, a month ago. Her boy was away at camp. A week in the wind, rain and cold as part of his education, I ask you! While he was away Mai went belly up after pinching more than her share of daily rations. They took her out, pushed and prodded but to no avail. I could have told them that she was a hopeless case. Ten minutes later I heard the toilet flush. What a dreadful way to go. I hope I do better when my time comes. Seems like the father wanted to warn Dean before he came home but the school advised against it: "Best break it gently…"

In the end that job was pre-empted by my boy, playing with his Lego when his brother came through the door, wet, smelly, cold and dying for some home cooking, clean clothes and a bath (yes, a small boy and I did hear him ask for a bath!)

"Hello Dean, your goldfish is dead!" Not "Did you have a good time?" Or "It's good to have you back…I've missed you!" Just a cryptic: " 'Lo Dean your goldfish is dead!" And fish are supposed to be cold blooded.

For a while I quite missed Mai Wong but grew to enjoy my own company as much as everyone else has always done. It was all going swimmingly (sic). I had more room in the bowl, it was cleaned as often and fresh gravel dropped in from time to time with some pondweed – I could almost forget that my home was plastic. Darren let Dean share the feeding and cleaning, so there was no rush to look for a replacement. Then it all started to get really hairy.

Father went off on a business trip and while he was away they overfilled my bowl. I didn't realise. Doing my isometrics one afternoon I flipped too hard and landed on the carpet. I lay gasping for breath and worried that I'd suffocate in the pile before anyone found me, though I needn't have, it was Cyril Lord for Buddha's sake! When she fetched the boys home from school and started to run the tap to wash some clothes or something Darren found me and I managed a faint curl to attract his attention, he yelled for help and the next thing I know she's picked me up.

"He's still alive." (Why are pets "He's" when humans can't tell the difference?) Suddenly I was plunged into a sink of boiling water!

My screams would have woken the great Chou. I think the steam and the flaking of my scales made her realise that something was wrong so she scooped me out in a cup and plunged me back into the icy waters of my bowl. It took my breath away so there were no more screams to disturb my ancestors.

We pedigree goldfish are resilient characters and after a few days moping at the bottom of the bowl I started to recover and all that's almost behind me now. I thought his comments were interesting when he came home from his business trip:

" Did you get him to confess? The hot and cold water treatment is an old Chinese torture used very effectively by the Germans during World War Two!"

He is a caring man but he was responsible for my next brush with death. All right, I know I shouldn't have flipped out again but I enjoyed a change of scene and was careful to make a decent splash and do it when one of them could hear or see. Not any more though. The last time I did it I disturbed something called a "Test Match" and he was not amused. So I feigned great weakness, barely managing to flip my tail.

"If he's (there's that masculine again!) been out a while we ought to do something to stimulate him," he said. "I know…"

Back in the bowl I was about to show increased life when I was doused with brown liquid from a bottle and the alcohol content of my swim went up. Before I knew what was what I'd swallowed great mouthfuls.

"It's OK dear," he said, "it's the Sainsbury's I give the Philistines who want mixers with their brandy."

Not even the Napoleon and I was already as drunk as a newt. I came through that and stopped having the hallucinations when they changed my water. I also stopped taking a walk on the carpet. I don't need telling twice!

I'm alive, well with no sign of permanent alcoholism but I'm worried witless. Chinese philosopher Confucius say: "Swinging chain sign of dead fish…"

Every time I hear the cistern flushed I lose another night's sleep…

By Alan Murton
Truro Creative Writers Group

Winning entry for category 7
Open Short Story
(Judged by Biddick Arts Centre Staff)

> *I love writing. I never feel really comfortable unless I am either actually writing or have a story going. I could not stop writing.*
> P.G. Wodehouse, English writer 1881-1975

The Hat

The hat shop was a secret delight. A relic of the days when ladies wore hats, it remained, hidden amongst "pound" shops and cut-price chemists, gleaming like an opal in the back street. Megan always looked in the window when she passed on her way to the market; and wondered how it survived. The displays were tasteful and discreet, a tribute to the lost art of window dressing, and the hats themselves, - Oh the hats! They were works of genius! Wedding hats that were an anthem of delicate shades and glorious blooms, funeral hats of sumptuous velvet with veils and plumes, summer hats that made the herbaceous borders look pedestrian and winter hats to bring colour and warmth to the coldest of pinched faces. Sadly, the prices were as exuberant as the hats, way beyond Megan's budget, but sometimes, in a moment of miraculous generosity, the unseen owner would display a "BARGAIN", and Megan would count her money, battle with her conscience, lose, and walk on, for hats were not a necessary. Just once, the day after her birthday, when she had money to spend, she had succumbed and bought a fantasy in longhaired lambskin, which made her feel like Julie Christie for a whole winter until the cat had kittens in it and it went into the bin alongside her youth.

The day was chilly and windy. "May!" thought Megan, "Feels more like November." She hunched into her thin fleece on her way to the market, head lowered against the flying dust. A crumpled piece of paper bounced erratically across the road in front of her and lodged in the gutter. She bent to retrieve it. A ten-pound note! She looked around and could see no one. The note could have blown from anywhere. It seemed like a gift from the fairies, as she stood there with it clutched in her hand. In front of her was the hat shop, and, there, in the centre of the window was a "Bargain". It was a wonder of a hat in shiny cream straw, with red ribbons and, heaped around the brim was a harvest festival of bright red cherries and glossy green leaves. It sang in the gloomy light and made her smile. The price ticket said "Today Only - £5". Before she was even aware of her actions she had bought it and salved her conscience by spending the rest of the money on a new dress for Moira, her daughter, and bedding for her expected baby.

Megan wore the hat throughout the summer, for in complete contrast, the next day dawned clear and hot, weather that continued through the following months. Megan glowed like the sunlight all summer, until the weather broke at the beginning of October, eight weeks before her baby was due. She was putting the hat into a carrier bag to put away for the winter, when she became faint and fell forward, burying her face in the folds of polythene. Her daughter found her, unconscious, when she came home from school. Megan was admitted to hospital suffering from oxygen starvation and remained there until after the premature birth of her baby Jason, a week later. The Hat was mislaid in the confusion. Megan found it again the following spring and, thinking to make a little money, took it to a local Dress Agency.

Meredith was looking for a wedding hat. She already had her outfit, bought for a twenty-first birthday; it would do very well for the wedding. It was, after all, merely a colleague from work who was getting married. Her reluctance to spend much money on a hat that would only be worn once led her to the Elite Dress Agency, where, on a shelf, rising above the fumes of dry-cleaning fluid and ancient perspiration, she found The Hat. The cherries were all wrong, of course, but the hat was in excellent condition and the ribbons were the right colour, so she bought it. Meredith considered herself something of a milliner and worked diligently to re-create the hat. Its ribbon rosettes and silk peonies won many admiring glances at the wedding, the only cloud being her inability to claim credit for the masterpiece, for she would not have wanted anyone to know that she had not bought the magnificent creation complete. When the wedding album was completed there were several photographs of Meredith in The Hat. She was flattered and delighted when the Office Manager complimented her on her taste and asked if she might borrow it to wear at a Woman of the Year Lunch the following month. Meredith took great pleasure in driving over to deliver The Hat, although the Office Manager lived some distance from town. On the way back she lost control of her car and hit a tree head on. She was found by a farmer early next morning, but it was already too late. The Office Manager was appalled and thrust The Hat out of sight into a wardrobe. The next spring she re-discovered it and, remembering Meredith's pride in it, sent it to a Charity Auction.

Martha recognised quality when she saw it. Most of the stuff at the Charity Auction was either blatantly vulgar or fashion tat, but the hat was well made, of sound material, and would last. She stripped it of all the fancy frippery, made a neat band and flat bow of navy-blue petersham ribbon and wore it to church every Sunday for five summers. Then, one chilly autumn evening, as she was putting the well-wrapped Hat away on top of the wardrobe, fell from the step-stool and broke her hip. She lay there, undiscovered, for three days. By the time the alarm had been raised by the milkman, she was dead. The hat, together with the rest of her good, well-cared for, sensible clothing was sent to the British Heart Foundation shop, where it was classed as "unseasonable" and put away until the following year.

Mandy was hot. The sun seemed to be captured and intensified by the shop windows, shimmering and glittering on all sides. "Must lose some weight," she thought, catching sight of herself in the window of a café. It was so overwhelmingly stuffy, and her feet, sweating in court shoes, ached. "I'll just have a cup of tea," she decided. Half an hour later she emerged full of Drinking Chocolate and Black Forest Gateau, feeling much happier. But her feet still ached. She minced to the charity shop window; perhaps they would have some strappy sandals in her size? Then she saw The Hat. That would keep her cool and look so elegant! The trimming was awful, of course, but the shop also had a fancy pink chiffon scarf and some silk roses that looked really lifelike, they even had imitation dew drops! She carried her booty triumphantly home, and went to work. She wore the hat all summer, at any excuse. She visited church fêtes and school galas. She spent her Sundays travelling to "Gardens- Open to the Public". She lost weight because she was so busy, and she met many new people.

One man, Geoffrey, was a keen gardener and they ran into each other at several of the venues. He bought her coffee and they talked. As the garden events drew to a close they visited the theatre together and discovered a common love of stage musicals. Mandy wore The Hat to go with him to an open-air production of My Fair Lady, and it was during the Interval that he proposed on the terrace. Mandy was so delighted that she leapt to her feet, then stumbled and fell over the low rail into the greenhouses below. When the police had finished their investigations and the tape had been removed from the scene The Hat was found by a gardener, tossed into a box of rubbish and sent to the dump.

The Dump was one of Maggie's regular stop-off points. Tom, who had worked there for many years, knew roughly when to expect her and would set aside any good clothing that came his way. He had no idea why Maggie had become homeless, they rarely even spoke, but, on her twice yearly visits they would share a pot of tea whilst sitting on a couple of old chairs he had pulled from the skip. Maggie would then retire discreetly behind his van and emerge in a magnificent, if ill-matched, set of new clothes. She would then toss her discarded garments disdainfully onto the garbage. On this occasion she halted in mid-toss and burrowed into the accumulated debris, to emerge clutching The Hat. "Look at this!" she exclaimed in an unprecedented burst of loquacity. "Lovely, this is!" The chiffon scarf remained, although its pink had faded to a deep cream, but the roses and ribbons had been pillaged. She plonked it on her head, collected her shopping trolley and set off again on her endless journey to nowhere. Some miles down the road she stopped to eat a packet of crisps that Tom had given her. While she rested at the roadside she broke off sprigs of hawthorn from the hedge, and, pushing the stems into the loosened straw, heaped a harvest of bright red berries and glossy green leaves around the brim. She never returned to the dump. Tom missed her vaguely and wondered, occasionally, what had happened to her, but the fisherman who found her beside a far-away river and the police who took charge of her battered body had no means of identifying her, or her acquaintance. No one saw The Hat as it fell into the fast-flowing water, no-one watched as it became water-logged and sank.

Moira was weary. Megan, her mum, had been ill for ages now, ever since before Jason was born, and now Dad had left. He had said that he was going South to look for work but they had heard nothing for months. Moira had noticed some women whispering in the playground when she went to pick up Jason and had tackled them. One of them, looking at her with the curious pity such women reserve for those they consider inferior, had told her that her dad had been seen in town with a young blonde. Moira did not feel any surprise. That was how things worked. She would go and get some veg from the market. They were packing up now so things would be cheap, then she would pick up Jason.

The day was chilly and windy. "May!" thought Moira, "Feels more like November." She hunched into her thin fleece, head lowered against the flying dust. A crumpled piece of paper bounced erratically across the road in front of her and lodged in the gutter. She bent to retrieve it. A ten-pound note! She looked around and could see no one. The note could have blown from anywhere. It seemed like a gift from the fairies, as she stood there with it clutched in her hand. In front of her was the hat shop, and, there, in the centre of the window was a "Bargain". It was a wonder of a hat in shiny cream straw, with red ribbons and, heaped around the brim, was a harvest festival of bright red cherries and glossy green leaves. It sang in the gloomy light and made her smile. The price ticket said "Today Only - £5". Before she was even aware of her actions she had bought it.

By Gael Shannon
(Associate Member)

Winning entry for category 8
Short Story Featuring 'Diamonds'
(Judged by Brian Lister)

> *O Diamond! Diamond!*
> *Thou little knowest the mischief done!*
> Sir Isaac Newton, English mathematician
> and physicist 1642-1727
> (to a dog, who knocked over a candle which set fire to some papers
> and thereby 'destroyed the almost finished labours of some years')

Hidden Depths

Looking into the heart of the diamond I felt my mouth drying, my stomach clench.

'Where did these stones come from?' I heard my voice demand, harsh, rasping.

'Hell.'

The reply barely penetrated my consciousness. Already I felt myself losing my grip on reality, plunging deep into the heart of the stone. White flames drew me into its swirling core and through the mists a face swam in and out of focus. Ice blue eyes bored into my soul, laying me bare. Every nuance of my character, favourable and flawed alike, was exposed. I saw myself clearly for the first time. No longer able to hide behind my subconscious. And what I saw terrified me. I knew beyond any doubt that I could kill, but worse, I saw that I could enjoy it. There was a part of me so savage and depraved it would sicken the most hardened criminal. I gloried in the pain I inflicted on others, relishing their fear. My blood quickened, my body hardened as the sights and sounds aroused me.

As I watched, the face I'd seen took form. I pulled my gaze away from her eyes noting her exquisite delicacy and innate sensuality. My eyes lingered on full round breasts and though the fabric of her dress concealed them, through some trick of my imagination I felt the sudden shock as, naked, her nipples pressed against my bared chest. I gasped and the eyeglass fell from my eye.

The uncut stone nestled still between my fingers and thumb and the voice of the man at my side reached my consciousness.

"Will you work on the stones?" His accent was thick and guttural.

I placed the diamond back onto the velvet cloth with the other two and looked up. His grey eyes regarded me coldly.

" Are you interested?" he asked, "because if you are not I can take them elsewhere."

"No!" My voice escaped me in a shout. "No," I said more evenly. "I think I might be interested."

The faintest sneer passed over his face, quickly replaced by a tight-lipped smile.

"Mr Goldbloom, I have come to you because you are said to be the best stone cutter in the world. You, I see, understand the unique quality of these stones. You alone, I believe, can cut them to reveal their inner heart."

His emphasis on the inner quality of the stones shot me back into their fiery depth. My mouth was still dry from the memory of those breasts. His words made me long for the opportunity to work on the stones and at that moment I would have given my soul for the chance to do so. My visitor coughed, abruptly severing the spell.

"Are you interested, Mr Goldbloom?" The question was clipped, sharp.

"Yes, what do you want me to do?" The words came from my lips but the hoarse voice was almost unrecognisable as my own.

• • • •

The sound of a car's wheels crunching on gravel, and doors slamming, brought me back to life. Since I'd had the diamonds my days and nights had been taken over by their potent spell. I was losing my grip on reality and I didn't care. I glanced out of the window and saw Yael's battered old car parked haphazardly by the front door. Irritation rose inside me and I wished I'd remembered to lock the house doors.

"Uncle Benjie, Uncle Benjie."

The voice rose through the empty house, young and joyous. Reluctantly I rolled the diamonds back in their velvet cloth and was bending over locking the safe when Sollie burst into the workshop. Seizing the moment, he leapt onto my back.

"Whee Uncle Benjie. Giddy-up, giddy-up." His little arms gripped my neck and his heels dug in. Laughing, I rose to my feet. Irritation vanished as I felt his hands, none too gently, patting my head while he crooned, "Good pony, lovely pony, giddy-up."

At four years old Sollie's zest for life was total. He did nothing by half measure. He was in love with life and threw himself into it with absolute commitment. He'd inherited this from his mother Yael. Seven years of marriage to my brother Solomon and two years of widowhood had dulled but not deadened her spirit. True to tradition their marriage had been brokered by a match maker. A union made in financial heaven to unite the two wealthiest families in the diamond business on both sides of the Atlantic. As a free-living, fun loving American, Yael had at first been amused by the self-righteous, pompous attitude of my older brother but, as the years passed and he became less tolerant of her marginally wayward ways, her feisty spirit had dimmed. Without Solomon, it was returning and I loved to see it.

Shortly after Solomon's death our mothers had tried to persuade us to marry - so I could look after my brother's family, they said. Yael had laughed her freedom-loving millionaire's laugh and no more had been said. We were good friends and if occasionally I felt a pang of sorrow that she didn't feel more for me, I never let it show, preferring friendship to nothing.

Sollie and I were galloping and bucking our way through the hall when Yael caught up with us.

"Whoa there, boy. Steady up now. Easy, boy."

I snorted and stamped as she approached. She rummaged in her pocket and brought out a sugar lump. Picking bits of hay and fluff from it she held it out to me, gentling me with her voice, holding my gaze with her own shining eyes. I snorted again and backed away, prancing sideways. Sollie's heels dug into me, driving me forwards. Whinnying softly I tentatively stepped to her. The sugar lump was raised. Our eyes locked together as gently my open lips brushed against her palm and took it. Her other hand rose to my cheek, caressing me, pushing the hair that had fallen forwards back behind my ear, lingering there.

"Good pony, good boy." Sollie's delighted giggles shattered the moment. I cleared my throat. Self-consciously, Yael brushed grains of sugar from her palm, a slight stickiness remaining from where my lips and hot breath had touched.

"Tea," I said abruptly, dropping my clinging passenger to the floor and propelling him to the kitchen.

"I'm gonna do lunch," Yael gathered herself with a display of domesticity.

"We've been out all day and haven't eaten a thing. Sollie's a hungry monster, aren't you pumpkin?"

Usually I loved her making herself at home in my kitchen. The big square room with its farmhouse table and perpetually burning Aga came alive when she inhabited it. Most days there was only me and a lot of empty space. She moved around it with easy confidence and I thought again how much this old house needed a family. Most of its days were spent in silent waiting. Sometimes I caught myself going to turn on the radio to break the loneliness, only to find it already on. Then, my emptiness was complete. Those were the days when work was going badly or inspiration just wouldn't come. Days when lumps of stone stayed silent, sullenly refusing to tell me their heart's desire. But since the diamonds had been in my possession those days had gone. Now my time was spent lost in their fiery hearts and at the deepest core of each the woman slumbered, waiting for my presence to waken her to some new depravity.

"We haven't seen much of you lately." Yael's voice coming muffled from behind the fridge door broke into my thoughts. "You eaten?" she added, peering round to look at me.

"No and no," I hedged, "just been busy with stuff."

"You've no food as usual, no wonder you're looking thin." She glanced up, concern in her eyes.

"I don't want any, I'm not hungry," I said perversely, "just do some for you and the kid."

My tone was abrupt and Yael's eyes flew to my face. I had never spoken to her like that before and I saw the hurt in her eyes.

"You're busy, we'll go."

I didn't stop her.

• • • •

Of the three stones I had only explored the depths of two. Her cold eyes challenging, the woman had led me and I had responded in ways I would never have believed possible.

The first stone showed me the foulest cruelties man could inflict. Drunk on the power the terror and pain of my victims built in me, I plunged in. Days passed in a haze. Inevitably the moment came when the arousal I felt through inflicting pain needed release. The blue eyes mocked me. I could see her clearly, but I couldn't touch her. The moment I tried I was slammed back into reality, blood pounding, my head exploding with pain.

The second stone held all the release I needed, and more. Full of sexual excess, every permutation of coupling, every conceivable sensual pleasure was lustfully enjoyed. And when the games of sexual cruelty took on a sinister tone the woman laughed with me and urged me on to blacker depths. I had felt her hot breath on my ear, heard her voice, soft and beguiling.

"The third stone Benjie, find me there."

Instinctively I moved to crush her to me and instantly was engulfed in the searing pain of awakened reality. It was at that moment I'd heard Yael's car on the drive and torn myself away. Now with Yael gone, I shakily unlocked the safe and drew out the third diamond.

The mists cleared immediately and the woman beckoned to me from inside a ring of people. The circle opened and I saw she was holding the hand of a small child. His welcoming grin shone out at me. I looked puzzled from the woman to the boy, wondering what place a child had amongst such players. A glance around at the lustful faces intent on the boy's figure informed me with paralysing horror.

"No," I pleaded, "don't do this, don't."

She laughed, her hands moving to the boy's shoulders, a sigh echoed from the throats around me. A low moan, a collective "yes."

"No, in God's name, you can't do this."

Her frosty stare froze me as her hands moved searchingly over the child's body. He, finally aware that something was amiss, tried to move towards me. The woman's cruel hands locked him to her as the circle closed in upon them.

"No," I screamed, "Oh God, Sollie, what have I done?"

I fought desperately with the crowd, trying with all my strength to part them.

"Uncle Benjie!" Sollie's terrified shouts tore into me.

I heard the woman's low laughter and a burning hatred filled me, giving me strength enough finally to burst through. I caught Sollie up in my arms, his pitiful naked body wracked by sobs of pure terror. Cradling him to me to hide his nakedness from their lascivious looks, my eyes bore into hers.

"Damn you to Hell," I shouted, "if you want him you'll have to kill me first."

"Oh yes," she moaned, moving towards me and at last I felt her hands upon me, snaking over me and the boy, burning us with their fierce desire.

"No!"

The agony that seared into me was familiar, not that of a crowd tearing me apart. I forced my eyes open and saw Yael kneeling before me, her face streaked with tears, her body shaking. Coming back to demand what was wrong with me, she had heard my ravings and had managed, in the nick of time, to swipe the diamond out of my hand, flinging it clear across the room. She held out her arms to me. Sobbing, I fell into them.

Hours later, from a small plane we scattered the diamonds over the dark waters of the North Sea. Slowly they moved with the waves, creeping closer to one another. One day hell would break loose again.

By Eve Gray
(Wear Valley Writers)

Winning entry for category 9
Short Story for Children
(Judged by Penny Dolan)

> *A children's writer should, ideally, be a dedicated semi-lunatic, a kind of poet with a marvellous idea...*
> Joan Aiken 1924-

The Calling

It's 3a.m. I'm sure I hear movement downstairs. I'm alone in the house. With shaking fingers I struggle into my dressing gown and slowly descend the stairs. The house is still, but I feel every nerve on edge. My ears are straining to catch the slightest sound. There is only silence. I reach out my hand. One more step down and I'll be able to reach the light switch. I take a deep breath and begin to move. My right foot steps into freezing cold water.

I should have known. It's come. I breathe in a cool dampness. It swirls like a living thing round the house, seeps under the floorboards, penetrates the very walls of my home. I expected the coming, waited longingly to recognise the signs, forgotten until now. Suddenly I realise I've lived for this moment. The promise is about to come true - the promise of long ago. I can almost hear Granny Seaweed's quavering voice.

"Yes, my lovey. You're not like other children."

I was a sickly child and knew I was different from others. I had to endure long spells in bed. Walking was difficult for me. The old seawoman, the one we called Granny Seaweed, came to keep me company while my mother was at work. She stroked my hair, her long gnarled fingers digging into my scalp. I flinched from her touch. Her bright almond eyes held me in their gaze. I felt myself melting into their dewy depth.

"Yes, my child. You are gifted. Your destiny is not of this world. Yours is in the unknown depths of the sea. You'll know when your time is come."

I drifted away, drowning in a blanket of enormous swirls of azure blue, weedy green, muddy brown. I was gasping for air. Suddenly I was in still water. A bright light drew me. I was floating on laughing sunlight-flecked waves. My heart burst with happiness. I wanted to roll, dive and frolic, but the dream faded as quickly as it came. I was back in my bed, held in the gaze of her dark shining eyes. I was afraid. I didn't understand the nightmares, the strange feelings she evoked in the depth of my soul.

Her hair, like wild streams of grey weed, hung in thick coils round her shoulders. Her voice rose and fell like the waves of the sea. Her hands, strong and gnarled like weathered roots, continued to stroke my hair. I was afraid of her walnut brown wrinkled face, the dark soft hair on her lip, her knowing smile.

"She's a witch," I told my mother, but she scarcely listened.

"Nonsense! Granny Seaweed's a dear old lady. She's kindness itself. She looks after you because she loves you. I know she looks a bit strange, but then she's very old. There's no one else who can spend time with you, darling. She means well so be thankful."

"But her stories frighten me. They make me feel strange."

But my mother smiled vaguely and turned away. She didn't understand.

The next time Granny Seaweed came to see me angry waves lashed the shore. The sky was filled with shrieking as gales thrashed the land. Trees crashed, boats were ripped from their moorings. I cowered under my blankets, afraid of the storm and afraid of the strange alien feelings that threatened to overcome me.

"Lock your doors. The water's rising. You may have to leave your homes for higher ground!"

But the storm passed. Old Granny Seaweed stroked my hair.

"Hush, my lovey. Don't be afraid. They are calling you, but it's not your time. You'll know. The call will be strong."

I was lost in her gaze. I had strange dreams, dreams of places far away and unknown. I heard sounds in my head, rushing sounds, gurgling sounds, whispering sounds. My body seemed to toss and turn, drifting, floating in some unseen embrace.

"When will I know, Granny Seaweed? Where must I go? I don't understand. I don't want to go anywhere. I just want to stay here, safe and warm."

"And so you shall. And so you shall. Nothing will frighten you when you are called. You will be strong when your time comes..."

I've waited for the calling for so long that I've almost forgotten. Old Granny Seaweed has gone. She disappeared one stormy night and was never seen again. Tonight I'm alone. I'm always alone. It seems I've waited my whole life for something to happen.

And now the cold water swirls around my ankles. As though in a trance I hobble towards the front door. The water sounds louder now, the call more urgent. I can't open the door. The pressure's too strong. Now someone is banging and shouting.

"Open up. You have to leave. The sea is rising."

The door is wrenched open. I'm almost knocked off my feet by the power of the icy water rushing into my house.

"Come along, Miss. You'll have to hurry. No time to lose."

I glance at the kindly man holding my arm. He's soaking wet and his lips are blue with cold.

I mustn't go with him. Suddenly I know exactly what I have to do. With almost inhuman strength I wrest myself from his grasp. He's staring into my face, his eyes huge with fear. I see myself reflected in them. It's not my face, but a nut-brown, wrinkled skin with long whiskers. I'm changing. My legs have disappeared. I look down in amazement at smooth black skin, and instead of feet I see flippers! No longer able to speak, I shake my head from side to side and dive into the rushing torrent.

My time has come. I must follow my destiny. With heart bursting with joy I swim and swim until the shore disappears from view. I keep swimming until I hear the voices - the voices of my people calling me, singing to me the timeless songs of the seals.

By Beth Daniels (Jersey Writers' Circle)

Winning entry for category 10
Non-Fictional Article
(Judged by Peter Barker)

 You don't write because you want to say something; you write because you've got something to say.
F Scott Fitzgerald, American novelist 1896-1940

Big Night At The Bridgewater

One night in January we go to a Concert. It's like many another night at the Bridgewater Hall - damp and dank the car park - icy cold the underpass - road and pavements treacherous. Careful not to slip. The homeless - a few of them - hold out their plastic cups to catch the rain. Hurry inside, before the cold and wet infect our spirits.

Poulenc tonight. We Senior Citizens are here in our thermals and in our legions. We have our season tickets - enjoyment guaranteed. There are young ones here - music-lovers like us, but perhaps not quite like us. Study the programme. Who's singing, who's playing? Scan the orchestra. The principal Cellist has had his hair cut - looks more like Rupert Brooke than ever.

The leader is in place. Jan Pascal Tortelier is wielding his baton. He mounts the rostrum and they're off. The starting gates are open and there's no question about who's leading. It's Poulenc. Belt and braces buckled. Take your seats for a ride around the Hall. Hold very tight. Doff your blouse and jacket for a frou-frou. Tousle your partner, show a little stocking, jostle that gent in the tweeds. We're gathering momentum, better hold on, we're about to corner at speed. Gosh, what a thrill - centrifuge for Seniors. Don't tell me Nanny didn't warn you. Too late for that, too late to go back, too late to stay in the century we were born in. That orchestra's a filly that won't stop careering until she passes the post. Jan Pascal demands a sharp rallentando, steady, hold hard, we're slowing, we're nearly at the buffers, we've stopped.

How was that for you, dear? Excellent! Me too. Shall we have ice cream or coffee? It takes us longer to get our ice cream here than ever it did in the Free Trade Hall.
What's next? What's for pud? More Poulenc, yum yum. A gorgeous soprano in a gorgeous blue gown and Jan-Pascal again, elegant as ever. Jan-Pascal, why not give us all a treat? Conduct your audience in a Latin-American fandango? Hush, hush! Do be quiet. They're beginning, and none of us wants to miss it. And he's French, you know, not Latin-American. We're all ready, poised for action. The choir inhales with its diaphragm - their voices will soar to the ceiling. The centre of gravity is up there in those spaces over the stalls and the stage and the rostrum. That's where it's happening, up among the lighting. That's where the Aliens will arrive and moor their invisible spacecraft when they come to witness the Awful Day. That's where the voice of the Recorder will sound, announcing the End of it all. That's where the Unseen Forces will gather to pronounce a terrible verdict on every man Jack of us.

But now the Conductor is rising into the air as if on a string, his coat-tails fluttering. The soprano soars beside him, her blue silk billowing, spinning around, like a doll in a musical box. Up goes the harpist, up with the angels, instrument aloft. Trombones after her, at maximum extension, floating flutes and piccolos, oboes and bassoons. Don't forget the strings, allargando, cantabile. They're building a crescendo, bowing out the Epoch. The horns are hell for leather, trading blows with trumpeters, watch out for percussion, there's going to be a crash. The choir comes in with a futuristic fugue. Each one takes his partner, fat, thin, bald, or hairy, high, low, bass profundo. To every man his part, every woman also. Sing for victory, sing for Salvation, sing for the hell of it.

Surely we can join them, leave the seats we've paid for, join the jubilation, the jolly goings on. Stately as our pensions we pace ourselves to Poulenc, and begin a graceful circuit of the auditorium. Not so stately, after all, not a bit, for Poulenc, albeit disembodied, swells with pride and has his way. We yield to him, obedient, and dance, like Coppelia, dance, dance, dance until we're dropping, dance, dance, dance because we must, until Doomsday. Keep to the right, keep to the left, dot those crotchets if you please. Wait for the crescendo, observe the rallentando, never mind the discord - it's good for the arthritis - the Music enters uncharted Spaces of the Universe. This is where it's taking us, all of us together, right now to the centre of it all. It's what we came for, we've arrived, we've arrived, as Poulenc intended.

The climax overwhelms us - Aliens and natives alike. Applause applause - Hurrah, hurrah for Poulenc, hurrah for the players and the Maestro and his Principal. Good show, good show, always better than before, again and again we iterate our encores. The orchestra shimmers down to earth, trapeze artists on silken ladders. It's over. The Choir mops its brow. Jan Pascal and the soprano, applauded enough, disappear behind and below to post-performance privacy.

For you and me it's 20-something minutes down the stairs into the street, where the rain still rains on homeless and homegoer alike. We search for our cars and set our sights on our front doors. That's it till February.

I can assure you that all this really happened. If you were there, I don't doubt you will have seen it.

By Joyce Neal (Telling Tales)

Winning entry for category 11
New 'Sitcom' or 'Soap' for TV

(Entrants were asked to submit their idea for the location, a list of the characters with a short biography of each, a brief synopsis of the first three episodes and a sample of dialogue from 3 scenes)

Humour is emotional chaos remembered in tranquility.
James Thurber, American humorist 1894-1961

'Whoppers'

The name for the sitcom is derived from its meaning in the context of 'fibs', 'porkies', 'little white lies' etc. To varying degrees, all of the characters are anomalies; they are normal people with (fairly) normal lives, readily identifiable with people we know, but there are surprises in store when circumstances cause them to divert from their usual path.

"Whoppers" is set close to a large city and the action primarily takes place in three houses which are situated on the outskirts. Two of them are in a very nice residential area; the other one is the much more humble (though very clean and neat!) home of the main character, in another district not too far away. Some scenes take place in restaurants and bistro type cafés in the city (those of the more 'up-market' type).

There is a link running through all 10 half-hour episodes, along with some story-lines which overlap and others which are completed in each episode. The main gist of the series is the unplanned realisation by Madge that she can secretly be 'someone else' for a few hours a week - someone with a more exciting lifestyle. This inevitably involves the telling of 'whoppers', though there is no evil deceit; neither is there any criminal activity. "It doesn't hurt anyone" is how Madge justifies her behaviour. The other characters all sometimes tell whoppers, too, and there are some rather surprising results.

New Anthology of Writing Gems

CENTRAL CHARACTERS

The women:
Madge Clipstone,
a cleaner

Celia Wilby-Drummond,
a barrister

Shirley Coombes,
a lady of leisure

The men:
Len Clipstone,
a carpenter

Miles Drummond,
a student

Major Harvey Bellingham,
a painter

BIOGRAPHIES

Madge Clipstone: Her full name is Marjorie Florence Clipstone but she has always been called Madge. She is in her 50s and is an intelligent, likeable, quite attractive lady, though she has 'let herself go' a little. She left school without any qualifications and has had no real desire or opportunity to alter the situation. She brought up three sons on a very modest income, all of whom now live long distances away. Madge has mostly worked in factories but for the past few years has preferred to do cleaning at 'posh' houses. She has earned herself a very good reputation as, apart from being an excellent, hardworking cleaner, she is completely honest and trustworthy. She currently works for two ladies: on Monday, Wednesday and Friday mornings for one, and Tuesday and Thursday mornings for the other. She enjoys the status of these jobs, in view of the fact that she is entrusted with keys to both houses, and that both of her employers treat her more as a confidante than a hired help.

Len Clipstone: Married to Madge for 30 years, Len is a carpenter with the local Council. He is quite a shy man and occupies himself a great deal by tinkering in his shed, making small items like bird tables and shelves for knick-knacks. (Their house and garden are somewhat overrun with examples of Len's handiwork!) He walks their dog twice a day and invariably arrives back at home carrying odd bits of timber or broken furniture, which he procures from any skips he happens to come across; he 'recycles' them.

Celia Wilby-Drummond: A very attractive divorcee, 40-something, Celia is a barrister and a staunch career woman. She blesses the day Madge came into her life. Celia is not very domesticated, and relies more and more heavily on Madge to sort out the running of her home - not just the cleaning of it three times a week. Madge does everything from feeding the cat (who would probably starve otherwise!) to making sure that the boiler gets serviced. Celia seems to have little time in her busy schedule for Miles, her son, but has relationships on the go with several men, though she takes none of them seriously.

Miles Drummond: Miles is twenty, studying dentistry at a college in the nearby city. He somewhat reluctantly continues to live at home rather than in student accommodation because it's convenient, though fraught with tension at times. He refuses to use the double-barrelled family name and very much plays down his so-called 'privileged' upbringing. He and Madge get on extremely well; she has almost assumed the role of grandmother in his life.

Shirley Coombes: Shirley employed Madge first and recommended her to Celia. They live on opposite sides of the street and are acquaintances rather than friends. The only thing they really have in common is the fact that Shirley's husband and Celia's ex-husband were at school together and have remained friends, though Celia's ex now lives with his new wife.

Shirley fancies herself as another Charlie Dimmock, in that she's always planting things and trundling a wheelbarrow around her property. She's very different from Celia in that she is usually seen in wellies and old clothes, whereas Celia is extremely smartly dressed at all times.
Shirley rarely sees Madge (hence having given her keys to the house) as almost every Tuesday and Thursday she 'goes out'. (More about that later!)

Major Harvey Bellingham: An imposing, good-looking, fit man of 60ish, of whom little is known at first. He doesn't appear until Episode 3, when it would seem that he is a retired military man, now a 'painter', who is reasonably well-heeled and who enjoys the company of ladies. It doesn't emerge until later episodes that he has no connections with the armed forces (or indeed the art world) - though he once painted the outside of an Army and Navy Surplus Store. He is, in fact, just plain old Harry Bell, a self- (but not very often) employed painter and decorator. He is not a criminal as such, but mostly just goes in for obtaining morning coffee in a smart bistro and lunch in an expensive restaurant, paid for by ladies he has managed to charm.

SYNOPSIS OF EPISODE 1:
The main character, Madge, is seen cleaning at Celia's house. Celia is harassed by her son's laziness and stressed because she is late for the office. Various things are seen going wrong, from the mildly frustrating to the calamitous.

Celia leaves. There are scenes with Madge and Miles together in the house, scenes with each of them on their own, and one of Celia at work. When Madge leaves, having finished that morning's work, she is seen talking to Shirley, who is in her front garden holding secateurs.

Madge says goodbye and is about to walk down the road to the bus stop when she remembers that she intended to take a suit of Celia's to be dry cleaned. She lets herself back into the house to fetch it, where it is lying on the bed. Miles has gone out by this time and then the life-changing moment happens for Madge! The ramifications of what Madge does in this scene provide the basis for the rest of the series. She is unaware of this though, as yet, and so is the viewer, though the seeds have been sown. She holds up the suit in front of herself, looks in the full-length mirror and likes what she sees. Madge gets a bus into the city and, instead of calling into the dry cleaners,' she buys a nice pair of shoes and a blouse in a charity shop. In the changing cubicle she dons Celia's classy suit and Episode 1 ends with her emerging, smiling, onto the street looking every bit the well-to-do lady on a shopping spree. Her 'other' clothes are in several bags with expensive store names on them, taken from a pile that has accumulated at the back of Celia's wardrobe.

SYNOPSIS OF EPISODE 2:
Madge's house features in the opening scene, and then Len is seen for the first time. He is trying to open the front door whilst battling with keys, the dog on its lead and a side rail from a baby's cot, which was once painted pink, but which now has most of the paint chewed off the top of it, from a succession of occupants.

Madge and Len's marriage is depicted throughout as a happy one, albeit rather humdrum! Len has settled down nicely into middle age without putting up a struggle, but we now see a very slight change in Madge. She is 'perkier', has pinned her hair up and is putting some lipstick on when Len comes in, though he doesn't notice. There is some debate on the usefulness or otherwise of one side of a cot and what it could be made into.

There are scenes of Madge at work in Shirley's house, scenes of chaos in Celia's (because Madge isn't there to deal with things) and a scene in which Madge and Miles secretly gang up on Celia. The closeness of their relationship takes on a new meaning in Episode 4, when Miles 'catches her out', though he plays along with her deception and the plot thickens.

The episode ends with Madge taking another deliberate step towards the double life she inadvertently sparked off at the end of Episode 1 - she is seen selecting another item to 'borrow' from Celia's extensive wardrobe and leaving the house with it in a bag.

SYNOPSIS OF EPISODE 3:

5 of the 6 main characters have been seen by this time and now the 'Major' makes an appearance. Madge is sitting outside a trendy bistro with a cup of coffee; she is looking immaculate in a trouser suit of Celia's that has not been worn for a couple of years. There are no empty tables so the Major invites himself to join Madge and immediately engages her in conversation. They establish their identities with each other, both telling 'whoppers' whilst sounding completely plausible. Madge is now Florence in this role.

The unthinkable happens when Madge spills coffee over one leg of her trousers. She tries to make little of it but later, at home, she attempts to wash it out and makes it worse - the material shows a distinct stain.

Other scenes show Madge at the cleaners', explaining about the stain, - ("Would you like the SOS Service?" asks the assistant. "That's Stains Overcome Superbly."), more strife between Miles and his mother, and Celia rummaging through her wardrobe. Madge, whose opinion is sought, steers her back to the 'recent stuff' end, and away from the 'what haven't I worn for ages?' end of the wardrobe, relieved that the missing trouser suit isn't thought of.

Meanwhile, Len has made what looks like a wooden TV aerial, from the baby's cot, but which is in fact a rack for drying home-made pasta. (Madge points out that they don't have a pasta making machine, nor are they ever likely to have one, but Len remains unconvinced. He says it's really easy as he's seen chefs make pasta in minutes on Ready, Steady, Cook.) Episode 3 ends with Madge collecting the trouser suit, having had to pay out a hefty amount for the SOS service, which thankfully did the trick.

SAMPLES OF DIALOGUE:

Madge: Celia, shall I go and wake Miles? It's half past eight and he's got lectures this morning, hasn't he?

Celia: HALF PAST EIGHT! Hell's bells, I'm due in court in an hour. NO! let me wake him, the lazy slob. I'll take his breakfast up to him.
(Madge looks surprised at this but Celia grabs a cereal packet and marches up to Miles' room)

Celia: Hi, Darling! Breakfast in bed for you today!
(Celia pulls back the duvet and proceeds to shake the box over her son, showering him with cornflakes)

Miles: MU-UM! I suppose you think that's funny?

Celia: It would have been funnier if I'd followed up with the milk and sugar! Clean up before Madge comes in.
(Celia then goes off to work, by which time Madge has prepared a tray of tea and toast; she takes it up to Miles, who is scooping handfuls of cornflakes from his bed)

Madge: Your Mum's 'room service' leaves a bit to be desired, doesn't it? Here, you eat this while I get the vacuum cleaner.

Miles: It's OK - I'll do it; she told me to clear it up before you came in.

Madge: *(with mock indignation)* And since when did you do anything your Mother asked? All right, go ahead then.

Miles: Er...Madge, ...where exactly do we keep the vacuum cleaner?

Madge: I rest my case! - Eat your toast!

• • • •

(from Episode 4)
Major Bellingham: Florence! How absolutely delightful you look today, my dear; lilac really suits you.

Madge: Thank you Harvey. I've always loved this outfit. Leonard bought it for me when we were last in Milan.

Major B: Ah, yes. Milan - a wonderful city.

Madge: Have you been there?

Major B: Hasn't everyone? *(Changing the subject quickly)* - Now, my dear, have you ordered coffee yet?

Madge: I was just about to.

Major B: Splendid. Would you be so kind as to order a cappuccino and a Danish for me? I must leave you for a few moments, my dear lady. I need to make a swift call to the auctioneer to see whether my bid was successful. I seem to have left my mobile in the car. Back soon! *(He departs long enough for Madge to have to pay for the pastries and coffee)*

Madge: So, did you get what you were after at the auction, Harvey? What was it, anyway?

Major B: Oh, just a rather lovely Victorian p...Florence, are you all right? *(Miles approaches their table outside the bistro and Madge nearly chokes from the shock)*

Miles: Mother! I thought it was you - no mistaking that lilac jacket, eh? *(Patting her back as she coughs and splutters)* Aren't you going to introduce me to your friend, - Mother?

Madge: Miles, f-fancy seeing you here! Er, this is...er...my son, Miles; Er...Miles, - Major Harvey Bellingham.

Major B: *(Shakes hands with Miles)* Nice to meet you, my dear boy. Fine looking young man, Florence.

Miles: Florence? Oh, no-one calls her that, Major.

Major B: No? *(Looking bemused, while Madge looks rather worried)*

Miles: No. *(Miles is having some sport with Madge now)* Everyone calls her...Marjorie, don't they, - Mother?

Madge: THANK you for that, Miles. Florence is my middle name but, yes, *(suddenly warming to the idea)* you may call me Marjorie instead, Harvey!

Miles: Just like everyone does, eh? - Mother? *(Madge relaxes and even manages a little forced laugh, now she knows that Miles is obviously enjoying the charade)*

• • • •

(from Episode 4)
Shirley: *(On the phone)* OK, thanks for letting me know; I'll see you at the usual time on Thursday then. *(Hangs up)*
Hi, Madge.

Madge: Oh, hello! I thought you'd be out as usual. It IS Tuesday, today, isn't it?

Shirley: Yes, it is, and I would have been, but he's…*(she was about to say 'he's had to cancel my lesson' but stopped herself short. She is secretly learning to ride a motorbike)* …he,… that is, my husband, says thanks for bathing the dog last Thursday, Madge. You're a real treasure.

Madge: Are you limping, Shirley? You are - what have you done?

Shirley: I'm fine, I just fell off the bi…the bed the other day. *(Not the best thing to say, in an attempt to cover up; it is generally assumed that she's having an affair as she's obviously 'up to something')* Well, when I say the bed I really mean the chair. I was standing on a chair to dust the top of the wardrobe and I fell ONTO the bed, then onto the floor. …And …hurt my hip. Yes, that's why I'm limping a little.

Madge: Mmm…dusting the wardrobe? Isn't that what you pay me for, Shirley? When you're in a hole it's best to stop digging, you know!

Shirley: OK, OK, - his name's Gareth, but I PROMISE you - it's NOT what you think!
(The two women laugh, then there is a scene change so Shirley's 'secret' is not revealed yet)

By Leona J Bryson (Associate Member)

Winning entry for category 12
Mini-Tale (up to 100 words on a postcard)

Brevity is the soul of wit.
Shakespeare (Hamlet act 2, sc.2)

All was still and calm in the lily pond. The frog surveyed her domain hoping to draw comfort from its familiarity. Ribbons of green swayed delicately to and fro; smooth, algaed hopping stones still led across the muddy bed; a goldfish darted in and out on his regular foray for food. Her frogspawn was safely tucked away below the bank. Daily the water became a little warmer. This should have been such a happy time. But without her mate, nothing was the same. Drat that interfering princess!

By Stuart Randall
(Moorside Writers)

Winning entry for category 13
Novel - any genre
synopsis and first 5000 words

> *'Oh! it is only a novel! . . . only Cecilia, or Camilla, or Belinda:' or, in short, only some work in which the most thorough knowledge of human nature, the happiest delineation of its varieties, the liveliest effusions of wit and humour are conveyed to the world in the best chosen language.*
> Jane Austen, 1775-1817 (Northanger Abbey)

Watcher In The Shadows

SYNOPSIS

Sylvie has a secret watcher. He keeps a daily vigil on the carefree teenager waiting for her return.

Her confidence knocked by yet another bloke letting her down, Sylvie is persuaded by her mother and family friend, Colin, to go with them to the village pub quiz night. Seeing ex-boyfriend, Paul, with his new fiancée doesn't help but she is befriended by Alan, a member of the visiting team. The watcher overhears their conversation at the bar and hurries out to the car park. On the way back to town, Alan's brakes fail on a sharp bend and the car crashes into an oncoming tractor, bursting into flames. On Tuesday evening, Sylvie waits in vain outside the cinema. Stood up again.

Fuelled by the dramatic results of his tampering and his escape from detection, the watcher's sense of power grows and his psychotic world takes over. His mission is to eliminate any newcomer who might sully Sylvie's innocence. Greg is jostled in the crowded railway station and falls under a passing train, Richard's body is found on the pavement at the foot of the multi-story car park and poor Guy hadn't even been a threat, Sylvie had turned down his invitation.

A new under-manager, Steven Lewis, is appointed to the Building Society where Sylvie works. Every instinct tells her to keep their budding romance a secret for as long as possible. Sylvie feels she is living a double life as the distance grows between the normal world with Steven and work in the town and the increasingly claustrophobic environment of the village with its strange characters like Tom Mapleton, landlord of 'The Red Lion', who fancies himself as a lady-killer, the monosyllabic Denis Crabtree who works in the Post Office, daft William who seems to have a crush on her and even ex fiancé, Paul.

When her grandmother is taken ill, her mother rushes up to Lincolnshire to look after her, leaving Sylvie alone. Sylvie spends more time with Steven, but she knows she must be careful. Steven spends many clandestine evenings at her house and eventually spends the whole night. The following evening, the watcher waits for Steven and tells him he has a message from Sylvie. Once tricked in to the watcher's house, Steven is at his mercy.

His dreams of the perfect, chaste girl waiting just for him now destroyed, the watcher's vengeance turns on Sylvie. In the early hours, she is woken by a noise. Someone is mounting the stairs. When he fails to cajole her into letting him in, he becomes demented and reveals he has Steven trapped. When he smashes down the door, Sylvie topples the wardrobe onto him. She races downstairs only to find the outer doors locked and the keys missing. Hearing him coming, Sylvie hides behind the kitchen door with a cast iron frying pan and hits him on the side of the head.

Steven, gagged and bound to the chair in the window of the watcher's attic room sees Sylvie running to discover what Colin has done to him.

CHAPTER 1

The street is narrow and badly lit. Strange shadows lurk in the lengthy stretches between the reluctant glimmer struggling from each streetlight. The oppressive silence of the late evening is broken only by the staccato double clack of the girl's stiletto sling-backs on the wet pavement. At the corner, she stops to look over her shoulder. The insipid yellow glow of the sodium lamp bleaches the colour from her face making her appear gaunt and haggard. She turns to stare into the dark recesses of the doorway of the long abandoned shop on the far side of the road. Her shoulders twitch as an involuntary shudder passes through her taut body. A thin drizzle begins to fall. She pulls up the collar on the short leather jacket, wraps its unfastened edges across her chest and hurries onward as though to escape from the long line of grey, empty eyed houses crowding in upon her.

He shivers too. But with excitement, not cold or apprehension.

It does not occur to her to glance upward. She does not see the slow twisted smirk spread over the long, cadaverous face watching from the unlit window. No one knows of the nightly vigil he keeps from the dormer window from where he can trace her journey along the whole length of the street. She has no idea about the fantasies he nurtures in his secret place as he waits for her passing.

She is gone now but he stays in his silent eyrie. He stretches out a spidery hand and with a bony finger writes her name in the mist his breath has generated on the icy pane of glass.

Sylvie looked around the room and sighed. Why had she let herself be talked into this? The place was full of old folk, just as she knew it would be. So much for all her mother's assurances about Tom Mapleton's plans to bring in the younger people with this new venture. There were several strangers, presumably members of the visiting team and their supporters, but none of them could be under forty either.

"You two find a table and I'll get the drinks. A shandy for you Margaret, and what will you have, Sylvie?"

"A diet coke will be fine." She was tempted to ask for a Bacardi in it but best not to scandalize the oldies. "So mum, where would you like to sit?"

"How about over there?"

Sylvie had no wish to be in the thick of things so was only too happy to squeeze her way through to one of the tables by the wall before the place got any more crowded. By all accounts it was going to be a busy night.

Without waiting for her mother who had stopped to chat with a friend, Sylvie hurried on to sit down before she became the centre of attention.

The small tables had been arranged in a series of decreasing semicircles facing the top of the room. At least Tom Mapleton had made an effort to make the place look festive even if it was more reminiscent of a wedding reception than a quiz night. Colourful banners and balloons hung from the ceiling and there were small vases of flowers dotted everywhere. Crisp white cloths covered two trestle tables set up at the front with pads of paper and pens laid out for each of the competitors. A large blackboard had been set up presumably to record the scores. At least, Sylvie thought to herself thankfully, the thing was not being held in the dingy, wood panelled main bar with all its dark corners and reeking of stale beer and ciga rettes. The function room, a 1960s addition, might lack character but it was at least light and spacious.

Sylvie took her time removing her jacket and arranging it over the back of the chair. Looking up, she was surprised to see Paul standing in the doorway. This sort of evening didn't strike her as the sort of event he'd be interested in. Just as she was about to give him a wave, he turned and spoke to someone behind him. It was a surprise to see him lead a mousy-haired girl to a couple of empty chairs in the far corner. The gossip had obviously been right. Paul wasn't exactly Leonardo DiCaprio, but you'd have thought he could have found himself someone a bit more attractive. It wasn't just that the girl was plain, she must have been several years older than him, late twenties, and that was being generous. Perhaps he'd learned his lesson about choosing girls who were too young to know their own minds, Sylvie thought ruefully. He was waving and smiling to various people who seemed keen to make themselves known. He must have brought her here to show her off to everyone.

"You're better off without him." Sylvie jumped. Colin was standing beside her. He must have seen the look on her face. "You don't want to let that Paul upset you. As I said to Margaret, you can do better than a car mechanic with no prospects."

"So it's you I've got to blame for turning mum against him is it?"

"What d'you mean?" His face took on the familiar pained look.

"Nothing." Sylvie gave a weak smile and did her best to look contrite. "Well, all that's history now."

She told herself not to be foolish. Why should she be resentful that Paul had found someone else? After all this time it was only to be expected and, as she was the one who had decided to end it all, she had only herself to blame.

"Good job we got here early. I told you they'd be busy." Colin put the drinks on the table and sat down in the adjacent seat.

Even if he hadn't been over liberal with the aftershave, surely a first for him, it would have been better if her mother had sat between the two of them. Not that anyone could possibly think that she was with Colin of course but, nonetheless, she would have preferred not to have been sitting alone with him.

"This is very pleasant isn't it? Great to see so many people here. It was good last time. You'll enjoy this."

"Umm." Sylvie edged away slightly as Colin pulled his chair nearer to the table.

"Tom said he's got Cyril in as extra barman for the evening so he can take a bit of time off to enjoy it all himself."

Unable to think of a suitable comment to what Colin obviously considered a significant development, Sylvie busied herself sipping her drink. Her mother was still gossiping with Mrs Nelson. "I think I'd better go and get mum. It's filling up fast. People keep looking over at the empty chairs at our table."

"No problem. Put your coat on that one next to you?"

Sylvie frowned. Surely he wanted her mother to sit next to him? "Tell you what, I'll shift round one and then I won't have to move it."

Tom Mapleton came into the bar and rang the bell.

"Right ladies and gents. We'll be starting in five minutes so if you'd like to get your drinks in, now's the time."

As Margaret Kilpatrick hurried over, Sylvie got to her feet to let her mother slide into the seat against the wall.

"I was just saying to Kathleen, good turnout, isn't it? It's a shame not to use this nice big room more often. I don't think I've been in here since we had that party for Alice and Harold's Golden Wedding last October."

Sylvie looked at her mother's slightly flushed face and shining eyes as she settled herself into the cramped space. Although she was pleased to see her so obviously enjoying herself, Sylvie felt a stab of guilt to realize how dull her mother's life must be that a poxy night out like this could make her so excited.

"Someone said that there was talk of the brewery wanting to turn it into a restaurant. Lots of the country pubs do very well apparently but luckily the idea didn't come to anything."

"I'm not surprised." Colin gave a derisive snort. "The locals wouldn't be interested and I can't see many Swinbourne people coming all the way out here. We're much too far off the beaten track. Anyway, they should keep the pub for the villagers."

Sylvie tried to suppress a giggle but not before she'd caught Colin's affronted gaze.

"I happen to think it's important to maintain our sense of village community. We're losing too many of our amenities. Look at that little grocery shop on Silver Road. It's been empty for months now. It's a long trek down to the Co-op. It's all right for those who've got cars. They can always go to the big out-of-town supermarkets outside. It's the old folk that suffer and them that have lived here for generations. We're fast losing our sense of identity."

"Lets face it, if Tom Mapleton had to rely on the likes of you and mum as customers, the Red Lion would soon go out of business. You know the saying, use it or lose it." She couldn't resist baiting him. Colin was far too young to start playing the pompous village elder.

As Colin sat tight-lipped, her mother cut in quickly, "Look, the teams are about to take their places. Although it's only a friendly tonight, if we do well, Tom's planning to see if we can enter the County League then we can have lots more of these evenings."

"If Arthur Watts and old Joe Parkins are the best we've got to offer, I don't think there's much chance of our lot winning do you?" Sylvie said with a laugh.

Her mother gave her a pained look. "What Arthur doesn't know about engines isn't worth knowing and Joe was really high up in that insurance company when he retired. And look there's Joyce Ainwright. You've got to admit she must have a really good general knowledge."

Sylvie smiled and nodded. She had a soft spot for the teacher who had made her days at the village Primary so enjoyable. She'd done well under her guidance but Sylvie had never been at ease in the massive West Swinbourne Comprehensive and she couldn't wait to leave. The careers teacher had tried to persuade her to stay on for 'A' levels, had even insisted on talking to her mother on one of the parents' evenings, but one of the few advantages of living in a village at least thirty years behind the times was that further education had never been high on the priority list, especially for girls.

"Good Heavens!" Sylvie sat upright with a start. "Surely Denis Crabtree isn't in the team. I've never heard the old misery say more than half a dozen words at one time."

Her mother gave a girlish giggle. She obviously found the thought of the monosyllabic postmaster taking part in the contest as bizarre as Sylvie. "It's all right. He's going to the blackboard. He'll be doing the scoring. Shush now. They're about to start."

There was a crush at the bar and Sylvie found herself being edged further to the side as more people elbowed their way through. She had to step back quickly to keep her balance and bumped into the person alongside her.

"Sorry." She turned and looked into the smiling freckled face.

"No problem. I think we might have a bit of a wait."

"As tonight's star, you ought to get preferential treatment. Congratulations by the way. You were really impressive. Good enough for Mastermind."

"I was just lucky." He gave a self-effacing grin. "They just asked me the right questions tonight. I'm only one of the team reserves really. Gordon couldn't make it so I had to step in at the last minute."

"Well, I bet Loxford are glad you were here this evening. Although I have to admit that our lot didn't put up much of an opposition." She raised her eyes in mock horror at the abject failure of the home team. He laughed and pushed back the stray lock of overlong fair hair.

"I'm Alan Conrad by the way. You live in the village?"

"Sylvie Kilpatrick. Born and bred here, I'm afraid."

"Seems like a nice place."

"Not bad if you like peace and quiet, but you have to go all the way into Swinbourne to get any action."

"You work there too?"

"Mmm. In the Wessex Building Society on Regent Street."

"That big glass-fronted place opposite Debenham's? There's always a steady stream of people in and out." He gave her another lopsided grin that made her heart give a little fillip. "Must keep you pretty busy all the time."

"I'm not out on the front desk so I don't deal much with customers but it can get a bit hectic behind the scenes, even with so many of us." Sylvie racked her brain to think of something more exciting to say. She wanted to keep him talking. Her mind went blank. In the end all she managed to say was a predictable, "So what do you do?"

CHAPTER 2

The two tall figures at the bar stand out from all the others. From across the room, he watches her. He sees the sparkle in her eyes as she looks at the young man nonchalantly leaning back to rest an elbow on the bar. Even at this distance, he can hear the tinkling laugh she gives in reply. Though the room is hot and clammy, a sudden chill shudders down his spine. His insides shrivel, gripped by the squeezing hand of dread, and momentarily he cannot move.

What right has this incomer? How dare he monopolise his Sylvie? He watches the upstart offer to buy her a drink and, with easy assurance, signal to the barman. There is a pain in his temples, a terrible pounding blotting out everything else around. He needs to lie down, close his eyes until the needle darts of light stop flashing behind them, but he has no choice. There is no option but to go over and eavesdrop on their conversation. He must know. Fulfil his mission.

His limbs feel heavy, like walking through water in slow motion, as he shuffles to the bar twisting a path through the labyrinth of crowded tables. He has to concentrate on the action of every step as if his legs had forgotten their normal function.

The two of them are so engrossed in each other that they take no heed of anyone else. Sylvie doesn't even realise that he is now standing behind her, so close that he can smell the newly washed chestnut waves that tumble to her shoulders. The sheen plays across its ripples every time she moves her head, turning it from lustrous bronze to fiery copper then burnished gold. It's all he can do not to lean forward and bury his face in the thick tresses.

The man's voice intrudes upon his reverie bringing him back sharply to the pain of reality. From over her shoulder he stares up at the handsome tanned features. The bright hazel eyes in the perfectly proportioned face are riveted on her, drinking in her every word. She calls him Alan. Tells him how impressed she was with all his answers on the Pre-Raphaelites in the second half of the quiz. Art was her favourite subject at school she says. If she'd stayed on, she would have done Art or Art History at 'A' Level. Alan smiles and the two of them talk about Dante Gabriel Rossetti and William Morris and names he's never heard of like Burne-Jones, Millais and Holman Hunt.

He can see Alan is impressed. Doesn't expect a village girl to know about such things. Despite himself, he smiles. He'd always known his Sylvie is special.

She is talking again. There's been a school trip to this big house out at Buscot and she'd fallen in love with these pictures, based on Sleeping Beauty, that went all round the walls of this big room. She couldn't get over the faces, sad and serene. Her art teacher was into all that she says and when he talked about the artists and what they were trying to do it was easy to see what he was on about.

They talk enthusiastically about the artist's love of detail, the depth of colour and the romantic settings. They are so engrossed they seem oblivious of the crowd around them. He feels the hurt, the sudden loneliness welling up inside of him.

When she turns her head, he can see that little lift of one eyebrow that she does when she's listening intently. That little quirk of hers that sends shivers of excitement down his spine. But that look should be kept just for him, not wasted on someone else. This worthless interloper who can't possibly appreciate its true value. It is all he can do to stop himself taking a swing at the smarmy, smiling face leering at his beloved, desecrating her with his lewd intentions.

He stands back a little to see her better and another eager customer edges between him and Sylvie to get to the bar. His hand is shaking as he picks up his drink and gulps it down. Doesn't she know he likes pictures too? He has them up on the walls of his special place. He can learn more if that's what she wants. He can swot up on these Pre-Raffle, whatever they are.

He has to wait until the customer has got his order before he can sidle close to her again. Best not to keep staring straight at them. Give away the fact that he is listening to their every word. If he positions himself carefully, he can see their expressions in the mirrored wall behind the rows of bottles. Now he is telling her all about himself. His love of racing and fast cars. All he has now is a '94 Golf GTi but one day, when he can afford it, he is going to get himself a decent sports car. A Porsche.

She turns a little and he can no longer see her face but he knows Sylvie is giving Alan admiring glances. She'd love to have a car, she says. As long as it's reliable, even an old banger would make an enormous difference to her life. Transport is so difficult living out in the sticks. Even getting to and from work can be a drag. The last bus back from town leaves just as the nightlife in Swinbourne gets interesting and you can't rely on lifts. She's really cross because this latest Sci-fi movie she wants to see has been moved to one of the smaller screens and doesn't start till gone eight which means she'd have to miss the end to catch the last bus.

He knows what's coming next. Naturally Alan loves Sci-fi too. They are both free next Tuesday.

Flame coloured lights spiral in front of his eyes and his vision is totally blurred. The pain that stretches across his forehead from temple to temple feels as though it is about to split his head right open. He is digging his nails into his clenched palms so tightly he almost breaks the skin. His jaw aches forcing him to stop grinding his teeth together. He begins to sway and has to clutch onto the bar to prevent himself from toppling over.

Last orders are called so the bar becomes crowded and he is jostled further away from the two of them. Now the hammer blows in his head become less urgent but why is everyone shouting and their words so unclear? Black shadows still come and go but thankfully clear vision returns, if only in snatches. He staggers to the door. He must get some air.

It's good to be in the quiet and out of the bright lights. The sharp cold gives momentary relief but his strength is gone. He totters to the low wall and collapses onto it.

Anger fires up again, deep in his belly. How dare he? This Alan character. Just because he's tall and good-looking he thinks every girl will fall into his arms. Doesn't the fool realise Sylvie is special? That she is too far above the likes of him and his ilk? He lifts his head to the sky and howls with the pain that is wracking every fibre of his being.

Exhaustion takes hold. His body sags. The pain eases and his mind gradually becomes clear again. He had managed to get rid of the others who had foolishly come between him and his Sylvie but this one deserves more than just a warning. More than the anonymous phone call. If he had a knife…

He stares at the line of cars parked on the Tarmac strip in front of him. There on the end is an L reg Golf. A slow smile creeps over his face. He'll show him. He'd teach this self-opinionated interloper that it doesn't do to come between him and his Sylvie. He will need to act quickly. The pub will be emptying in a few minutes.

Silently he crosses to the back fence and squeezes through the narrow gap left by one of the collapsing panels. No one hears the creak of the shed door or the clutter as he searches manically for some suitable tool.

Luckily, the key to the rusty old padlock on the tool shed round the back went missing last Easter and, as yet, no one's got round to replacing it.

"You coming Alan?"

He turned and waved towards the group assembling by the doorway. "Be there in a minute, Nigel. You lot go on."

Alan ignores the nudges and knowing looks the noisy crowd were giving and turned back to Sylvie. Now at last, they were the only two left in the room.

Before he could say anything, Cyril came through and pointedly pulled down the metal grill to seal off the bar. Sylvie jumped as it hit the counter with a loud clang behind her and they both turned to stare at the intruder, their intimate conversation no longer private.

"Night." Cyril grinned at them and cocked his head towards the door.

"We'd better go. They want to lock the doors and your friends will be wondering what you're up to." Alan thought he could detect a tinge of regret in Sylvie's voice.

They drifted out into the narrow corridor where they constantly brushed against each other as they tried to walk side by side. Only one small light was on in the main bar and the landlord stood holding open the main door, his face expressionless.

"Thanks. Goodnight."

Alan's pleasantries were ignored.

"Great evening, Mr Mapleton. Everyone enjoyed it."

The door was closed firmly behind them and, as they heard the sound of the bolts being sharply drawn across as though in condemnation, Alan pulled a wry face and shrugged his shoulders.

There were still several groups of people milling about outside, one or two were more than a little tipsy, although there was only one car left in the car park.

"Your friends seem to have gone without you," said Sylvie.

"I had to come straight from work so I came on my own anyway. Can I give you a lift?"

Sylvie shook her head. "It's not far. I walked down with mum and Colin so I expect they're waiting for me." She looked around and pointed to them out chatting with an elderly couple sat on the wall of the raised flowerbed planted around the post for the pub sign. "I'd better be going." She made no move.

In such a public place, all he could do was give her a broad smile. "You sure you don't want me to pick you up on Tuesday?"

"Loxford's right the other side of town! Much too far out of your way. It's kind enough for you to offer to bring me back after. I'll see you outside the cinema as we agreed."

"Till Tuesday then."

"Look forward to it."

He was as reluctant to wander back to the car as she evidently was to return to her mother. He turned and looked back before he opened the door. By the time he was in and had fastened his seat belt, the pub court yard was deserted and the little clusters of laughing and joking villagers were slowly on the move.

He waved a hand as he passed and watched her in the mirror all the way down the road as she continued to flap her arm up high in the air until he had rounded the corner.

Things hadn't turned out so badly after all. Funny how you had days like that. It hadn't started too well with him oversleeping and arriving late at work and when Alex Piggot had phoned to beg him to step in at the last minute he hadn't been in the least bit keen. He knew the folk in Chisleton had a reputation for being a bit simple, all that interbreeding so they said, but he'd thought that was just a joke. When he'd first arrived at the pub and discovered what a right collection of odd-bods they were, stuck in a time warp most of them, he wasn't so sure that the rumours weren't fully justified. And all so ancient! There couldn't have been more than half a dozen of them in the place under fifty. At least it had made the quiz a walk over and he'd done well. He'd been well proud of his performance. Probably get picked for the team if he could keep it up.

Still, meeting Sylvie was definitely the highlight of the evening. A real sweet kid and not bad in the looks department. Best to take things easy though. She might be naïve for her age but, whatever the rest of the villagers were like, she was no fool.

Chiselton lay off the beaten track, on the way to nowhere, so Alan was not familiar with the roads. It took far longer to get to the A418 than he'd anticipated and when he found himself driving into another village, he realised that he must have taken a wrong turning somewhere along the way. At the crossroads in the centre, he let the car drift to a stop and got out to read the words carved into the wooden direction arrows that his headlights had failed to pick out with any clarity. Why, he demanded of the deserted streets, couldn't the county council or whoever had responsibility for such things, put up decent road signs as in every other civilized area? It didn't help his temper to discover that he was now further from Swinbourne than he'd been when he'd left Chiselton.

He set off again with a screech of tyres but soon found himself having to slow right down to take the succession of bends in the narrow road that snaked round the fields bounded by trees and straggly bushes. He knew he was driving much too fast but the temptation of a straight stretch of road proved too good to pass up. The lights from another vehicle still hidden by the high hedge flickered at the next bend. The bank of black and white chevron markers made him ease up further on the throttle, but he was still going too fast to take the sharp lefthander. His foot jabbed at the pedal.

The panic hit him like a fist between the eyes. He stamped hard. Again and again. Nothing. He pushed both feet to the floor, body arched. The bend still rushed towards him. The bright lights, oh so close.

From then on, everything happened in slow motion. He had time to register surprise when the tractor came into view. Why on earth was anyone out with farm machinery so late at night? There was a brief moment of relief when he worked out that it would clear the corner before he got there. At worst, he might get away with just ploughing through the hedgeway on the far side. That was before he realised that the tractor was pulling a massive load of hay.

The car hit the trailer broadside. The impact was deafening. His body rocked violently, the back of his head ricocheted against the rest. Time stopped. The front of his car was a mess but at least he was all right. Perhaps it was too early yet for pain. He should feel his legs, check nothing was broken.

That was when the bales tumbled down from above encasing him in a suffocating cocoon, blotting out what little light there was.

More noise. A roar, then snapping and crackling. And light. Bright, flickering light. Red. Orange. Flame. And then there was the smell. Before he could work out what it reminded him of, there was a great whoosh. Noise, light, smell. Altogether.

And then came the agony.

By Judith Cranswick (Penpushers)

Winning entry for category 14
The Denise Robertson Silver Trophy for the Best Group Anthology

Room 14 at 8 o'clock

By Richmond Writers' Circle

The Richmond Writers' Circle has met regularly in Richmond, Surrey, for over 50 years. Their anthology is the work of current members and is the first to be produced in book format. Its contents have been chosen by two editorial teams, one for poetry and one for short stories, ensuring that the best work of the circle is represented.

For many years, the Richmond Writers' Circle held its weekly meetings at the Richmond Adult Community College - in Room 14 at 8 o'clock.

Copies of the anthology are available from:
The Chairman, Richmond Writers' Circle
c/o The Old Vicarage
173 Kew Road
Richmond
Surrey TW9 2BB

email: rwritersc@yahoo.co.uk
website: www.envy.nu/rwc/Writers.html

Room 14 at 8 o'clock: (Extracts)

The Birthday Card

If you'd seen me you would have been wondering why I was sitting on a stone cemetery wall which ran down one side of a road of rather dismal terraced houses. The sky was overcast and it was drizzling. My gaze was fixed on number 43 opposite. But the dusky dark green painted door stood closed and the grey lace curtains bespoke a house of neglect. Perhaps a widower? But I was there today, this particular day, because this was the one day in the year that had really mattered to both of us.

Mind you it was a very brief relationship (as they call it nowadays). Two years' courting and two years' wedded bliss. So it took four years for us to discover we were not suited - I believe incompatible is the word they use now. Not like these film stars and footballers - four weeks if they're lucky. The funny thing is we may have been incompatible, but we were still in love.

But to return to the date - it was the day of our shared birthday. So we always remembered it. At first, after we parted, we exchanged cards - "Thinking of you" and that sort of thing.

But then I remarried and my hubby was a bit resentful of this card arriving each year. Silly, really, but there you are - anything for a quiet life. I stopped first so he couldn't blame me, but after two or three anniversaries his stopped as well.

This was all a very long time ago, but now in the last years of my life it kept coming to the forefront of my mind. It became almost an obsession. I found a snapshot of us and wondered how he looked now. And then I looked at myself - that made me have my hair done and buy myself a new coat. I wouldn't admit to myself why I'd done that. What had happened to him? Was he still alive? The address I kept was a hundred miles away. This year I made up my mind to go

North and see if he still lived in the same house. I knew it was highly unlikely and yet I knew he was always a stick-in-the-mud; he probably stayed in the same district for fifty years. That was what made him and me fall out. I wanted to go places, travel, but of course I never did. Jim, the children and lack of money (in equal proportions) made sure of that.

So here I was, sitting on a damp wall trying to pluck up courage to cross the road and knock on the door of number 43. I'm not sure why I needed courage - I suppose I was frightened that I should hear that he had died and his widow would look me in the face and want to know what I wanted. I sat there for about two hours until passers-by began to look at me curiously and curtains twitched at the next door neighbours' houses, and then I slowly made my way back to the station. And I must admit that in the train back I couldn't stop a few tears trickling down my cheek. It's amazing how long love can last. It came back to me just as if I was still seventeen.

I live in sheltered accommodation and the other residents are very nosy - they don't go out much and so curiosity is their form of entertainment. As soon as I put the key in the door a head popped out from Number 19. "Where've you been?" she said. "There's been a gentleman looking for you. He waited for ages. He even had a cup of tea in Mabel's flat. In the end he had to go. But he's left you a lovely Birthday Card."

By Pamela Risner

Song of the South River

Adapted from the classical Chinese of Li Yi (769-827)

I married the busiest of merchants.
Each morning I sat and my time was my own.
Now by the river I watch every tide

for his sail to return and still all my time is my own.
Better for me to have married that boy
Who returns with his boat on each tide.

By Harry Garlick & Chan Ching-wah

Relationships

A relationship is like a jigsaw puzzle.
You have it all worked out, fit the last pieces together.
Stand back, enjoy the whole.
If you look too closely, though,
All you will see is a multitude of cracks.

By Nancy Godwin

Through The Wire

Looked across the fence,
One end of summer afternoon,
Smiled, and met the neighbour:

Secateurs and roses, heavy headed red velvet
Pulsing with life. Her gardening glove
Exposed tattooed numbers: blue grey
Ink fuzzing with age. Six digits? Seven?
So many deaths in those blurred figures.

In Streatham at teatime on a T-shirt day
Dachau opened its eyes and stared
From behind a fence. Its wires slashed
Between us, electric, uncrossable. Inside,
Was a lond-dead pre-war Poland, perfect
To the last detail of wooden panels,
Stove and icons - a last defence

Held, somehow, through every horror
And rebuilt.

Those blurred blue grey numbers
Veiled the house and made it
Holy, a living cenotaph
With roses.

By Owen Wheatley

Teamwork

Wheel to leisurely wheel they cycled
To Teddington - Tide-ending-town.
Along the towpath riding races
With butterflies and thistledown.

The river singing, up from the city,
To see what there is where there is no sea,
The water running bright as sunshine.
Just him and her; just he and she

As lovers will, they murmured daydreams
Tracing hopes as lovers do
Sharing prospects for the future
Stardust talk of dreams come true.

She said: 'Broad-ranging corporate vision
Can neutralise strategic threat
And bring niche market domination.'
He said: 'I love it when you talk like that.'

He said: 'Co-operation is the future
Synergy the way ahead.
Let's form a market coalition.'

She said: 'Let's be teamwork led.'

Thus they came to form a merger
Expansion plans were soon pursued
And following incorporation
Small subsidiaries accrued.

Alas! In a while, boardroom schisms
Began to cloud the idyllic scene
Replacing 'ours' with hers-and-hisms
The heavenly contract contravened.

Her lawyers called him on his mobile
And told him that his day was done
Another's bid had been accepted
Their message was: 'Don't try to run.'

So sadly now he cycles solo
Wondering how his project failed
Was his leadership defective?
Had some glass ceiling at last prevailed?

And the river runs and the tide turns
And there are salty tears where there is no sea
And maybe dearest we should note this motto.
It isn't teamwork - it's thee and me.

By Mike Gordon

There were two things about which Martin Hogarth's friends were in complete agreement. The first was that Martin was the most affable man one could wish to meet; the second was that his behaviour before Christmas every year was distinctly and unaccountably odd. The arrival of Advent had, for as long as any of them could remember, always signalled the end of Martin's cheery demeanour and the onset of a gloom which, as the festivities approached their climax, became deeper and more profound.

This had often been a source of some ribaldry between said friends, for it is well known that Martin always spent Christmas with his relations. How awful his family must be, they thought, for the prospect of a single day in their company to manifest such a remarkable change in such a sanguine personality.

This year, however, they felt sure would be different, for Martin's mother, his last surviving relative, had died suddenly that summer from a heart attack after inadvertently sitting on a wasp, and Martin, a confirmed bachelor, would for the first time be at a loose end over Christmas. So, as December approached, offers came from friends far and wide inviting him to spend Christmas in their company. To their surprise though, Martin politely but steadfastly refused all such invitations, and remained doggedly tight-lipped about what his holiday plans might be. More significantly, his mood towards the end of the year, far from improving, became even gloomier than usual, and it began to occur to his friends that Martin's annual Yuletide misanthropy might not be connected with his family after all.

In this, however, they were quite wrong, for Martin's family were indeed the cause of his festive misery, and this despite the fact that they were, or had been, quite the nicest, most cheerful, uncomplicated family one could wish to have: loving parents, fond grannies and grandpas, delightfully eccentric uncles and aunts positively tumbled over themselves in Martin's family tree. No. The problem was unique and stemmed, Martin firmly believed, from rash words spoken as a small child one Christmas dinner. It was, he had long and grimly supposed, a testimony to either the power of prayer or God's warped sense of humour that his youthful entreaty on that distant Christmas Day should have been so literally interpreted and acted upon. There could be no other explanation.

His enthusiasm for Christmas in those far gone days had been extraordinary, even for a small child, and not without good cause. For the Hogarth family Christmas was so jolly, rumbustious, and awash with sentiment that even Dickens would have been made nauseous. It had been during such a Christmas, when he was five or six years old, that the fateful words had been spoken. The adults had laughed affectionately at his sweet innocence, then thought no more of what he had said, and indeed Martin himself had no recollection of his request until some years later – when it started to happen.

It began with Uncle Hubert. Uncle Hubert was Martin's favourite uncle, his father's elder brother, a jovial reprobate of enormous appetite who, though in his fifties, seemed to Martin at times barely older than himself: a child in an adult body, a man of whom Peter Pan would have been proud. Uncle Hubert was the perfect uncle, a living Father Christmas, who every year could be guaranteed to bestow upon Martin whatever his current heart's desire might be. He was also, unfortunately, a man who lacked the bodily constitution to withstand the overindulgence to which he daily subjected his poor frame, and at the tragically early age of 54 he succumbed to a fatal heart attack. Martin was 14 and devastated.

And so Christmas that year had, for the first time, a more sombre air than usual. In remembrance of dear departed Hubert, a commemorative place was set for him at the dinner table and, before the family sat down to partake of the traditional fare, they hung their heads in a minute's silent tribute to their late beloved relative. During this hiatus, Martin prayed with childish fervour that Uncle Hubert, wherever he was in the Great Beyond, was also having a good Christmas. It came as a considerable surprise therefore, when the silence ended and he raised his head, to see sitting before him none other than Uncle Hubert, in his customary place, sipping his customary Madeira, grinning his customary jaunty grin. Grinning, moreover, at Martin who, after gaping open-mouthed for a few moments at the friendly spectre, immediately closed his eyes and shook his head to clear the impossible vision from his senses. When he opened them again, however, Uncle Hubert, to his amazement, remained stubbornly imposed on his retina. He instinctively glanced round to ascertain whether the rest of the family were experiencing the same incredible phenomenon, but it was immediately apparent from the ordinariness of their manner that they were not, and Martin realised with a shock that Uncle Hubert was making this startling appearance solely for his benefit.

'You were very quiet over dinner,' his father commented after the meal. Hubert, to Martin's relief, had by this time disappeared.

'I was thinking of Uncle Hubert,' Martin replied truthfully.

'Yes, indeed,' said his father wistfully. 'Poor Hubert. Still, he wouldn't want us to be glum over Christmas on his account, would he?'

'No,' said Martin, 'he wouldn't.' Martin had paused a moment and considered his next words with care. 'You didn't. . . see anything odd at the table, did you, dad?' he asked tentatively.

'What do you mean?' queried his father.

'Oh, nothing,' said Martin. 'It's just that I. . . well, I thought I. . . oh, never mind,' he muttered, realising from his father's look of puzzled innocence that he had, quite clearly, seen nothing.

During the course of the next year, Martin gradually forgot about his experience at the Christmas table, dismissing the incident as an hallucination, and the following Christmas he sat down to dinner in his customary place, confident that the extraordinary occurrence of the previous year would not be repeated. As his father carved the turkey however, there, suddenly, standing at his shoulder, smiling benignly at Martin with a ghostly glass of Madeira raised in salutation, stood Uncle Hubert, and Martin began to get an ominous feeling that, in future, Christmas would never be quite the same again. And so it proved. On Christmas Day from that time onwards, as the family sat down for dinner, Uncle Hubert would make his annual appearance to Martin, Madeira in hand – followed by an occasional spectral cigar – the ghost of Christmas past. In the course of time Martin became almost accustomed to this unsettling manifestation and, though he was not afraid, he definitely began to wish that Uncle Hubert would spend his Christmas dinner elsewhere. He would have dearly liked to broach this delicate subject to Uncle Hubert, but Martin was very aware that Hubert appeared only to himself, and that to engage his uncle's ectoplasm in conversation would certainly excite comment from his other relatives at the table.

Then, one year, when Martin was in his mid-twenties, towards the end of Christmas dinner, the ghostly Hubert, circumnavigating as was his wont the festive table, suddenly stopped behind the chair of old Grandma Hogarth, and, smiling sadly, shook his head and gently laid a phantom finger upon her shoulder. Martin, who was of above average intelligence, knew a sign when he saw one, so it came as no surprise to him when, later the following year, the angels clasped old Grandma Hogarth at last to their bosom. Next Christmas dinner, when Uncle Hubert arrived to bid Martin cheery greeting, he was not alone.

And so Uncle Hubert, now accompanied by old Grandma Hogarth, continued to haunt Martin's Yuletide meals. Years passed, and as the foothills of middle age encroached upon Martin's horizon, Uncle Hubert began increasingly to lay his spectral hand upon the shoulders of Martin's ageing relations, a sure sign that the following year there would be one less mortal at the dinner table and one more spook.

It is said that a man can get used to anything, and to an extent this was true of Martin, but by the time he was forty the number of dead relatives at his Christmas table outnumbered the living, and he felt the situation was getting out of hand, particularly as it was becoming increasingly difficult to pretend to his few living relations that he was not surrounded by a ghostly crew of extinct ones.

But it was when Uncle Hubert, in his role of jovial Grim Reaper, laid his dread hand upon the shoulder of Martin's father (who, though in sound health at the time, died some weeks later in a bizarre gardening accident) that Martin finally decided enough was enough. Determined to ring the changes, he spent the following Christmas abroad, where he was confident Uncle Hubert, old Granny Hogarth et al would not follow. Even in a remote part of Denmark, however, where he was staying with an old friend, there was no escape, for even as he sat down on Christmas Day to a traditional Scandinavian repast, there, amid the exotic patés and pickled herrings, appeared the familiar shape of Uncle Hubert, followed in quick succession by the rest of his supernatural family, now including, he was grieved to see, his father. They all appeared disconcertingly at ease with the change of continent, and with sinking heart Martin realised that there was to be no escape, either now or in the future, from his annual ordeal.

That had been five years ago. Now his mother was also gone and, as the last of the Hogarths, he would for the first time be entirely alone at Christmas. He considered fasting for the day, if only to confuse Uncle Hubert's schedule, but decided that this would be to no avail, his phantom family was sure to appear anyway. Then suddenly it occurred to him that here was the chance he had been looking for: he would take this opportunity to break his long held silence, talk to Uncle Hubert, and plead with him to end the dismal Yuletide hauntings that had plagued him for so long.

And so, alone in his flat on Christmas Day, he prepared a modest meal and awaited the familiar arrivals. No sooner had he sat down at the table and raised his knife and fork than the entire ghostly crew, with Hubert at their head, congregated claustrophobically around him.

Martin, steeling himself for the confrontation, got shakily to his feet and addressed them, his voice a mixture of frustration and entreaty.

'I didn't mean it, you know,' he croaked. 'What I said all those years ago – as a child. How could you have taken me so literally?'

There was a slight pause. Uncle Hubert smiled his big Father Christmas smile and spoke.

'But of course you meant it, Martin,' he said. 'You were a little boy, my favourite nephew, and I could never deny you anything you wished for so passionately.'

'I take it back,' Martin said desperately. 'I don't want you to visit me any more. It's driving me mad!'

'You don't mean that,' chuckled Uncle Hubert. 'And anyway, you can't take it back. What's done is done. Your wish was granted. You wished – and I can remember it clear as day – that we, your dear, dear family, would always be with you at Christmas. For ever and ever.'

'But I'm alive and you're all dead,' cried Martin. 'I don't want to be alone with a family of ghosts!'

At which Uncle Hubert turned to Martin's parents, grandparents, uncles and aunts, who all smiled sympathetically at Martin, realising that he meant what he said, and meant it just as much as he had meant his childish entreaty forty years earlier. As if in silent agreement, they nodded at Uncle Hubert who, grinning his customary jaunty grin, turned back towards Martin and, stretching out his arm, gently touched him on the shoulder.

By Kevin Buxton

Judge's Comments

Category 1. Free verse Poem (Katrina Porteous)
Free verse is poetry made from the diction and rhythms of everyday speech. I had to disallow several entries in this category because they used patterns of rhyme, which could not qualify as free verse. Poems in blank verse (a regular pattern of iambic pentameter) are not free verse either, even though unrhymed. For this reason I excluded poems wholly in blank verse, but included those which varied passages of blank verse with unmetrical lines. These caveats aside, the standard of entry was extremely high. I particularly like the winning poem, *'Harry's Spirit Level'*, because it anchors the emotions of love and loss in a particular object. I admire its economy, its play of sound, and the clarity of thought and feeling in the short sentences which close it.

Category 2. Sonnet, Villanelle or Pantoum (Alison Chisholm)
A *'Dear John' Villanelle* exhibits mastery of a difficult form, and offers an ideal subject for the haunting quality and the continuous assertions of the refrains. It is technically excellent, making good use of the two rhyming sounds to ensure a natural 'voice' speaking throughout the poem. It tells the reader plenty about the situation, and relies on simple, direct statements to describe the scenario. The repeated lines appear with identical wording, but by clever use of grammar and punctuation they are given different nuances with every hearing. The form underpins and never dominates the poem, which is as accomplished as it is compelling. A worthy winner!

Category 3. Poem For Children (Mavis Carter)
In judging this category, I was looking for not only well-constructed poems but originality of subject matter as well as rhythm and the use of humour.

It was a pleasure to read and re-read the entries over a period of weeks. The winning poem, *School*, and the other three finalists are a joy to read and I would love to have written them myself.

Category 4. Love Poem (Dave Etchell)

Having agreed to judge the Love poems I was not sure what to expect; being brought up on the classic love poems of Shakespeare, Burns, the Brownings etc., I certainly knew what I liked. The most difficult part , in the absence of any quantitative methodology, meant that I was reduced to that most irrational means of final selection - my personal feelings about the poems! But in the end I felt I had no option other than to have joint winners- one rhymning, one unrhymned. It was a very close run thing and I must thank all who took part for much enjoyment in reading their poems.

Category 5. Poem which can be sung to a well-known tune (John Chambers)

The new category of Best Poem Which Can Sung To Well Known Tune was an unknown quantity. What first surprised me was the range of topics and emotions covered by the entries, from the sublime to the gor(e) blimey, with a real bias towards the humorous, but the real cruncher was that the winner should be a hymn! A beautifully crafted piece with excellent phrasing, the words fit the tune exceptionally well.

Category 6. Monologue (Val McLane)

The standard of entries in the monologue category was exceptionally high and it was very difficult to choose just one winner, but for originality and wit it had to be *'Talking Goldfish Head'*. The writer of this monologue grasped the dramatic techniques of suspense and surprise as well as writing in a quirky but hilariously funny, accessible style. The work was entertaining and clever, beautifully crafted and a delight to read.

Category 7. Open Short Story (Biddick Arts Centre Staff)

As usual the standard of entries was very good. One story, however, stood out from the rest - *The Hat*. It was a very well written piece with plot and good story development. The style was very reminiscent of the work Roald Dahl used to do for Tales of the Unexpected. A definite winner.

Category 8. Short Story featuring 'Diamonds' (Brian Lister)

I was immediately impressed by *Hidden Depths*. It had a strong opening; without preamble it took you straight into the action. There was some bold writing that might have offended a few sensitive souls but was, quite correctly, included. A surreal story, using Jekyll and Hyde imagery that is outwardly entertaining and yet, for the reader, unsettlingly accusatory. A clear winner in my estimation.

Category 9. Short story for Children (Penny Dolan)

Writing children's stories isn't an easy option. It's not enough to have a good idea; you need to edit as if you were a poet, 'see' the scenes as if you were a dramatist and re-write with the passion of a perfectionist. Children deserve that much! *The Calling* keeps it simple but tells it well; it is the strange mix of menace and attraction that make this hauntingly atmospheric story into a very strong tale for slightly older children. It might be worth thinking around names a little more; the 'Granny' is fine but I'm still not sure about the 'Seaweed'. Nevertheless, a gripping piece of writing that drags you in!

Category 10. Non-Fictional Article (Peter Barker)

The entries were of a high standard and I had the pleasure of reading many interesting pieces. Throughout my professional life as a broadcaster I have had to use words, not only to convey precise meaning, but also to engage the attention of a listener, and a successful piece of prose must take one's mind to another level, towards the realm of imagination and individuality. The winning entry, *Big Night at the Bridgewater*, certainly did this, making what could have been an unremarkable, ordinary experience into something quite out of this world.

Category 11. New 'Sitcom' or 'Soap' for TV (Ken Rock)

Situation comedy is probably the most difficult form of writing of all. It is very structured and almost always follows a similar formula.

Whoppers has strong, well-defined and well-developed characters that gives opportunities to bring out their traits through the circumstances in which they find themselves. The storylines are interesting and have potential for lots of laughter. The sample script and dialogue is correctly laid out but I would have liked to have seen samples from the same episode rather than bits from two different episodes. However, this was a new idea for the Competition and uncharted waters are always precarious!

Whoppers does not fall directly into the sitcom format and is probably more suited as a comedy drama. However, with a little more work it could be developed to fit into a sitcom format.

Category 12. Mini-Tale
(Some members of the NAWG Committee)

In previous years the short-listed Mini-Tales have been judged by attendees of the annual Festival of Writing held in Durham; however, in order to complete this anthology in time to launch it immediately after the Competition Awards Ceremony it was necessary to decide on the winner in advance! As with all the other categories, the judging was done with complete anonymity, and Stuart Randall's amusing little tale was the unanimous choice.

Category 13. Novel (Iain Pattison)
Watcher In The Shadows

This is the rarest of all creatures - a thriller that actually thrills. From the opening page this suspense story grabs the reader and won't let go. It's a genuinely creepy, tingling read packed with menace and malice - the sort of novel that is uncomfortable to read but impossible to put down. I really felt I was reading a proper book, not just a competition entry.

Category 14. Group Anthology (Souvenir Press Ltd.)
ROOM 14 AT 8 O'CLOCK

Well-considered production and design; obvious editorial thought went into the selection and a number of excellent contributions. (*'Song of the South River'* by Harry Garlick and Chan Ching-wah stood out, as did the ghost story by Kevin Buxton.)

NAWG Annual Creative Writing Competition 2002

Results

(In alphabetical order, not order of merit)

Category 1: **Free Verse Poem (Judged by Katrina Porteous)**

Finalists: Barry Adams (Inn Scribers), Penelope Alexander (Wellingborough Writers), Maggie Spooner (Wilmslow Creative Writers' Group), John Statham (Alsager Writers' Circle).

Highly Commended: Lesley James (Inn Scribers), Stuart Randall (Moorside Writers), Dorothy Walker (Irwell Writers).

Category 2: **Sonnet, Villanelle or Pantoum (Judged by Alison Chisholm)**

Finalists: Jane Lawson (Associate Member), Lilian Butler (Nene Valley Writers' Circle), Jane Harland (Congleton Writers' Forum), Diane Impey (Market Rasen Writers' Group).

Highly Commended: Rosy Machin (Lewes U3A Writing Group), Mrs P Netherclift (Wessex Writers' Group).

Category 3: **Poem For Children (Judged by Mavis Carter)**

Finalists: Julian Budden (Congleton Writers' Forum), Alison Read (Yeovil Writers' Circle), John Statham (Alsager Writers' Circle), Mike Wilson (Free Spirit Writers).

Highly Commended: Hilary Adams (Keele Writers), Nick Brigham (Newcastle College Creative Writers' Group), Aine

Maire Chadwick (Will Power), Jeanne Ferguson-Sykes (Heritage Poets), Vivien Hampshire (Phrase Writers), Austin Lawrence (Filey Writers), Jean Penn (Ass. Member), Stu Phillips (Kessingland Writers), Angela Pritchard (Alsager Writers' Circle), Cathy Rushworth (Norwich Writers' Circle), Gill Smith (Reading Writers' Group), Ed Turley (Wear Valley Writers).

Category 4: **Love Poem (Judged by Dave Etchell)**

Finalists: Rob Blaney (Alsager Writers' Circle), Janet Fielding (Congleton Writers' Forum), Lesley James (Inn Scribers), Mary Smythe (Lewes U3A Writing Workshop).

Highly Commended:
Leona J Bryson (Ass. Member), Dorothy Cooke (Moorside Writers), Morag Hadley (Ass. Member), Sheila Irving (Wyndham Writers' Group), Susan Mary Peterson (The Write Stuff).

Category 5: **Poem which can be sung to a well-known tune (Judged by John Chambers)**

Finalists: Barry Adams (Inn Scribers), June Davies (Associate Member), Bill Thomas (Keele Writers' Group), Mike Wilson (Free Spirit Writers).

Highly Commended:
Colin Ferguson (Thames Valley Writers' Group), Pamela Liebeck (Keele Writers' Group), Gael Shannon (Ass. Member), Hilda Slater (Thursday Fourum), Maggie Spooner (Wilmslow Creative Writers' Group).

Category 6: **Monologue (Judged by Val McLane)**

Finalists: Joyce Hicks (Waveney Writers' Circle), Alan Murton (Truro Creative Writers' Group), Joyce Robinson

(Thames Valley Writers' Circle), Sonia Royal (New Coast Writers' Group).

Highly Commended:
Barbara Maitra (Blaydon Writers), Julia McBride (Ass. Member).

Category 7: **Open Short Story (Judged by Biddick Arts Centre Staff)**

Finalists: Beth Daniels (Jersey Writers' Circle), Don Longthorp (Truro Creative Writers' Group), Anne Powell (Lewes U3A Writing Workshop), Gael Shannon (Associate Member).

Highly Commended:
Nick Brigham (Newcastle College Creative Writers' Group), Linda Ewles (Mendip Writers), Ted Harrison (Ass. Member), Pamela Howarth (Harrow Writers), Marjorie Major (Thursday Fourum), Jim Pearson (Foyle Street Writers), Brian Webster (Ass. Member), Diane Wilson (Free Spirit Writers).

Category 8: **Short Story featuring 'Diamonds' (Judged by Brian Lister)**

Finalists: Eve Gray (Wear Valley Writers), Simon Varley (Harrow Writers), Diane Wilson (Free Spirit Writers), Jenny Yates (Irwell Writers).

Highly Commended:
Aine Maire Chadwick (Will Power), Pam Dickinson (Wilmslow Writers), Edward James (Ass. Member).

Category 9: **Short Story For Children (Judged by Penny Dolan)**

Finalists: Beth Daniels (Jersey Writers' Circle), Lois A Johnson (Writers Reign), Celia Meade (Writers Reign), Mike Wilson (Free Spirit Writers).

Highly Commended:
Penelope Alexander (Wellingborough Writers), Aine

Maire Chadwick (Will Power), Pam Coveney (Ass. Member), Robert Heath (Matlock Writers), Jean Penn (Ass. Member).

Category 10: Non-Fictional Article (Judged by Peter Barker)

Finalists: Morag Hadley (Associate Member), Joyce Neal (Telling Tales), John A Silkstone (Market Rasen Writers' Group), Dorothy Walker (Irwell Writers).
Highly Commended:
Elizabeth P Berk (Thames Valley Writers' Circle), Jean Currie (Ass. Member), Marion Hayes (Nene Valley Writers' Circle), Celia Meade (Writers Reign), Yvette Verner (Uckfield & District Writers), Fred Vernon (Northampton Literature Group).

Category 11: New 'Sitcom' or 'Soap' for TV (Judged by Ken Rock)

Finalists: Leona J Bryson (Associate Member), John Statham (Alsager Writers' Circle),
John Talman (The Untapped Writers), Ted Warner (Lincoln Phoenix Writers' Circle).

Category 12: Mini-Tale (10 Short-listed entries)

Kirsty Adlard - Fosseway Writers, Lois A Johnson - Writers Reign, Kay Knutsen - Lewes U3A Writers' Workshop, Barbara Maitra - Blaydon Writers, Nimmi Rajiv - Writers Reign, Stuart Randall - Moorside Writers, Hilda Slater - The Thursday Fourum, Jacqueline A Smith - Associate Member, Maggie Spooner - Wilmslow Creative Writers' Group, Diane Wilson - Free Spirit Writers.

Please note: In previous years, Festival attendees have voted for their favourite Mini-Tale. This year we hope to have some copies of the Winners Anthology available immediately after the Awards Ceremony, so in order to include the Mini-Tale the winner had to be chosen before the Festival. Five members of the NAWG Executive Committee voted from the short-listed entries and the winner will be announced during the ceremony as usual.

Category 13:　Novel (Judged by Iain Pattison)

Finalists:　　Judith Cranswick (Penpushers), Ghislaine Davies-Goff (Barrack Road Writers), Jean Hughes (Dialstone Writers), Sheila Jackson (Hertsmere Writers' Circle).

Highly Commended:
　　　　Helen Corcoran (Ass. Member), Sally Spedding (Barrack Road Writers), Maggie Spooner (Wilmslow Creative Writers' Group), Peter Wynn Norris (Barrack Road Writers).

Category 14:　Best Group Anthology (Judged by Souvenir Press Ltd)

Finalists:　　Pennine Ink Writers' Workshop, Richmond Writers' Circle, Truro Creative Writers' Group, Wellingborough Writers.

Highly commended:
　　　　Barrack Road Writers, Lincoln Phoenix Writers' Circle.

Jayne Osborn
(Competition Administrator)

New Anthology of Writing Gems